DEANE-PETER BAKER is a Senior Lecturer in the School of Humanities and Social Sciences at UNSW Canberra, the division of UNSW Australia that is the academic service provider to the Australian Defence Force Academy. A former army officer who served in the British Army and South African Army, Deane is a philosopher who now specialises mainly in military ethics. He also teaches and writes in other areas, including strategic studies and public policy. In addition to his role at UNSW Canberra Deane holds the position of Visiting Research Fellow in the Department of Philosophy at the University of Johannesburg and is also a researcher in the Australian Centre for the Study of Armed Conflict and Society (ACSACS). He taught previously at the University of KwaZulu-Natal (South Africa) and in the Department of Leadership, Ethics and Law at the United States Naval Academy.

Key Concepts in
Military
Ethics

EDITED BY DEANE-PETER BAKER

UNSW PRESS

A UNSW Press book

Published by
NewSouth Publishing
University of New South Wales Press Ltd
University of New South Wales
Sydney NSW 2052
AUSTRALIA
newsouthpublishing.com

This work © University of New South Wales Press Ltd 2015
Photographs © Deane-Peter Baker 2015
First published 2015

10 9 8 7 6 5 4 3 2 1

National Library of Australia
Cataloguing-in-Publication entry

Title: Key Concepts in Military Ethics / Deane-Peter Baker (editor).
ISBN: 9781742234380 (paperback)
    9781742242132 (ebook)
    9781742247472 (ePDF)
Subjects: War – Moral and ethical aspects.
    War (Philosophy).
    Military ethics.
    Ethical problems.
    War and society.
Other Creators/Contributors: Baker, Deane-Peter, editor.
Dewey Number: 172.42

Design Di Quick
Cover design Xou Creative
Photographs Deane-Peter Baker

A horse stands near a lonely grave on Spioenkop, site of a major battle of the Second Anglo-Boer War that took place on 23 and 24 January 1900.

CONTENTS

Dr Deane-Peter Baker on board a Bell UH-1 'Huey' military helicopter.

INTRODUCTION

DEANE-PETER BAKER

When those of us who work in the field of military ethics are asked in social settings about what we do for a living, our responses are met, more often than not, with bemusement and comments like 'I didn't know there was such a thing' or 'Isn't that an oxymoron?' There's something in these responses that recognises a truth: the nature of military force and its application gives rise to contexts in which the requirement to act ethically can be very challenging, and there are numerous examples of military failure in this regard. On the other hand, there's a certain irony involved in this knee-jerk scepticism about the idea of military ethics. That's because the core foundations of military ethics, the principles known collectively as Just War Theory, are among the most pedigreed and well-developed sets of ethical principles in existence. Just War Theory is also arguably unique in being a fully-fledged and distinct ethical framework that applies to just one area of human social activity, the use of military force. Other professions that take ethics seriously, such as the medical profession, primarily apply general ethical concepts to the specific issues being addressed – they have no profession-specific framework comparable to Just War Theory.

One reason that the idea of (say) medical ethics is generally received with less bemusement than the idea of military ethics is that people outside of the medical profession are generally far more aware of the work that goes on in the medical profession to ensure ethical behaviour by medical professionals. Who hasn't heard of the hospital ethics committee? This familiarity is in part because ordinary members of society are much more likely to have some direct experience of the medical profession than of the internal workings of the military. For obvious reasons the military profession is in general less 'outsider friendly' than the medical profession (though, as discussed in Chapter 11 the military is often less outsider friendly than is necessitated by issues of operational security and the like), and the likelihood of an ordinary member of society having any dealings with a military ethicist are slim indeed. Still, this lack of public awareness is unfortunate, and it is our hope that this book will do something towards addressing it.

At this point I should probably make a clarification about what I mean by the term 'military ethicist'. There are a good number of very respected and highly qualified academics, most of them philosophers, who work on issues related to the military profession and military uses of force, many of whom I would nonetheless not consider to be military ethicists *per se*. Here I cannot do better than to quote the 2010 article by the editors of *The Journal of Military Ethics*, Martin L. Cook and Henrik Syse, entitled 'What should we mean by Military Ethics?':

> We are often put in circumstances of hearing philosophical talks. Often these are wonderfully logically developed, conceptually clear, rigorously argued and in the end professionally irrelevant. In other words, papers in which philosophers argue with the positions of other philosophers, no matter how interesting they may be by the canons of the

discipline, are not really military ethics in our sense. The test is fairly simple here: is what's going on in this paper the sort of thing that might be helpful in providing real-world guidance for policy-makers, military commanders and leaders, or operational decision-making? (Cook and Syse 2010, 120)

All the contributors to this book are, at the time of its publication, part of the teaching and research team in the School of Humanities and Social Sciences at UNSW Canberra, the Canberra-based campus of UNSW Australia that is responsible for all of the degree programs offered to the Cadets and Midshipmen of the Australian Defence Force Academy (UNSW Canberra is co-located with ADFA). As such we're a group of scholars who take the professional relevance of what we teach and write about very seriously indeed. Our exposure to military life has not only come vicariously through our Cadets and Midshipmen – several of the contributors to this volume have themselves had distinguished military careers, with operational and advisory deployments into hot spots from Afghanistan to Bosnia-Herzegovina, East Timor and parts of Africa. UNSW Canberra is rightly recognised as Australia's centre of excellence for military ethics teaching and research, and as among the top global institutions in this regard. Our goal in this book is to communicate some of the central concepts that we teach to our students to a broader audience of military personnel and others who would benefit from an accessible resource outlining the fundamentals of military ethics. We take it that this latter category includes policy-makers, journalists, NGO employees and anyone who takes seriously the idea that citizens have a responsibility to understand the military that serves them and what parameters define appropriate military action. The book is also intended to serve as a companion volume to an exciting new UNSW Canberra venture, a MOOC (Massive Open

Online Course) called 'Ethics for the Military Profession: An Introduction'.

Because of our commitment to providing real-world guidance to our students and the broader community of military and policy leaders, we tend to define the notion of military ethics somewhat more broadly than most. For many, the idea of military ethics begins and ends with questions related to the application of military force on the battlefield. While this is obviously the central pillar of ethics as it relates to the military profession, we are also acutely aware that many (perhaps most) of the ethically challenging decisions that must be made by military professionals relate to more mundane but nonetheless ethically important questions such as how to relate to subordinates and superiors, justice in the allocation of resources and goods, issues related to military procurement, and the like. As such we place significant emphasis on the application of general ethical principles to issues in military life as well as on the military-specific principles of Just War Theory. Likewise we take seriously the societal context of the military profession, which is important to understand properly for many of the ethical decisions that must be made by military professionals and related policy-makers. As a consequence the chapters that follow begin with a section outlining important foundational ethical theory, followed by a section concentrating on the societal context in which the military operates and the ethical implications of that context. We then move on to a section addressing broad ethical issues that arise within the everyday world of the military, before addressing, in parts four and five, many of the key issues that fall under the broad umbrella of Just War Theory. As an acknowledgment of the fact that the character of war is continually changing, we end this book with a section addressing some of the key emerging challenges that today face military professionals and their civilian masters.

I would be remiss not to acknowledge that, since Michael Walzer's ground-breaking book *Just and Unjust Wars* was published in 1977, awakening the discipline of military ethics from a long slumber, several excellent books have been published addressing aspects of military ethics or providing detailed overviews of the field (I hope I will be excused for perhaps a touch of bias if I say that *Military Ethics: An Introduction with Case Studies* by my colleague Stephen Coleman (2013) – a contributor to this book – is among the best, if not *the* best, of the latter category). Many of those books are referenced in the pages that follow, and the volume you are currently reading is not intended to compete with or replace any of those excellent works. Instead, we saw the need for a book offering a concise and accessible account of key issues in military ethics, to serve as a ready and quick guide to any interested reader, whether a member of the military profession or not. In order to keep our chapters short and focused we have majored on the concepts under consideration and largely set aside the historical context of what is covered. For the same reason we've not employed in-depth case studies to draw out the application of the concepts and issues in this book – that has already been done with great skill in the two books mentioned earlier in this paragraph as well as several others, and we felt there was no need to reinvent the wheel. Instead, the goal of this book is to offer a foundational account of central issues, and it is our hope that many readers will continue on to explore them in more depth (the 'References and further reading' section at the end of each chapter is designed to aid you in this).

Overall, our hope is that this volume represents a small contribution to erasing that sense of bemusement that many experience when they are confronted with the notion of military ethics. But most of all we hope that you, the reader, will find this book to be *useful*.

References and further reading

Stephen Coleman. 2013. *Military Ethics: An Introduction with Case Studies*. Oxford University Press.

Martin Cook and Henrik Syse. 2010. 'What should we mean by military ethics?' *Journal of Military Ethics*, 9 (2), pp. 119 – 122.

Michael Walzer. 1977. *Just and Unjust Wars: A Moral Argument with Historical Illustrations*. Basic Books.

PART ONE
FOUNDATIONS

The Parthenon in Athens, Greece.

1

ETHICAL DILEMMAS AND TESTS OF INTEGRITY

STEPHEN COLEMAN

Ethics is a branch of philosophy which examines questions about human conduct, specifically addressing questions of what is right and wrong, just and unjust, virtuous and non-virtuous in such conduct. Thus many questions or claims are, in one way or another, issues of ethics. For example, a person who asserts the claim that 'might makes right' is making a statement about ethics, as is a person who claims that it is acceptable to lie in certain circumstances, as is a person who suggests that abortion is always wrong.

Any decision which involves an ethical component is an ethical decision (i.e. it is a decision about an ethical issue) and that is what I mean when I use the term in the following discussion. It is important to be clear about this point, since this usage of the term doesn't necessarily match up to everyday discussions. If, for example, a person says something like, 'Bill made a very ethical decision when he reported his supervisor for harassing that new employee', then they are clearly using the term 'ethical decision' as a shorthand for 'ethically correct decision'. However, there can be good ethical decisions and there can be bad ethical decisions, so in this discussion the term will be used simply to refer to a decision which has an ethical component.

Given that an ethical decision is a decision which has an ethical component, and that ethics addresses questions of right and wrong in human behaviour, it should be obvious that ethical decision-making is something everyone is actually very familiar with, whether they are aware of this or not. A decision to participate in a protest about a newly proposed government policy is an ethical decision, as is a decision to knowingly falsify an income tax return, as is a decision to tell a cashier that they have given you too much change after your purchase, as is a decision to go to war.

While ethical decision-making is something everyone engages in, not all ethical decisions are equally important. In the decisions mentioned above, telling the cashier they having given you too much change is obviously a pretty minor decision, while going to war is equally obviously a very serious decision. In the same way that some decisions are more important than others, some ethical decisions are more difficult than others, and it is important to note that there are two, quite distinct, ways in which difficulty might arise. When faced with, or examining, a difficult ethical decision, it is important to understand where the difficulty lies, since recognising this helps to clarify the problems involved in the decision. The first way in which an ethical decision might be difficult is because it is very hard to work out what the right thing to do actually is; this might be because there are a lot of competing considerations, all more or less equally important, or it might be because every option in a particular situation is a bad option. The second way in which an ethical decision might be difficult is because it might be hard, for a range of reasons, to actually *do* the right thing, and this sort of difficulty can arise even when it is perfectly obvious what the right thing to do is. Difficult ethical decisions of the first sort, when it is hard to work out what the right thing to do is, can be referred to as ethical dilemmas (or sometimes, as a test of ethics). Difficult ethical decisions of the second sort, where it is hard to *do* the right thing, can be referred to as tests of integrity.

Tests of integrity and ethical dilemmas may be equally difficult to deal with, but the difficulty in each of these situations lies in a different area. In the case of an ethical dilemma, the difficulty is in deciding what the right thing to do is. In the case of a test of integrity, the difficulty lies not in deciding what the right thing to do is, but in actually doing it. Sometimes a particular decision might involve both types of difficulty, so even after resolving the ethical dilemma (that is, working out what the right thing to do is) a person is still faced with a test of integrity (difficulty in doing the right thing). However, most problematic ethical decisions do fit relatively neatly into one of these two categories.

It might seem a little odd to suggest that a generally good person might have difficulty in doing the right thing, but there are a range of reasons why it may be difficult for a person to do what they know to be the right thing in a situation where they are faced with a test of integrity. It may be, for example, that doing the right thing is unpopular, either with that person's friends, family or peers, or with the community at large. Or it might be that there is a lot of pressure, in one way or another, placed on that person, to not do the right thing, in that they might be bribed, bullied or blackmailed. The person might have a lot to gain from not doing the right thing, such as significant financial rewards, or the person, or those close to them, might have a lot to lose from the person doing the right thing in this case. But if someone knows what the right thing to do is, but finds it difficult to actually do the right thing, then they are facing a test of integrity, whether the difficulty is caused by pressure, or the chance of gain, or any of the other reasons just mentioned.

References and further reading

Stephen Coleman. 2009. 'The Problems of Duty and Loyalty'. *Journal of Military Ethics* 8 (2), pp. 105–15.

Stephen Coleman. 2013. *Military Ethics: An Introduction with Case Studies*. Oxford University Press, pp. 1–7.

CONSEQUENTIALIST ETHICS

DEANE-PETER BAKER

For many people today, when faced with an ethical dilemma, their intuitive response will be to weigh the consequences of each possible course of action against one another, and choose the course of action which results in the best overall consequences for all the people affected. Perhaps without realising it, those who make their ethical decisions following this intuition are applying the central tenet of an ethical system called *utilitarianism*, a form of *consequentialism* developed in England in the 18th century. There are other approaches to ethics that focus on consequences, or contain some element of consequentialism, but utilitarianism so dominates this approach to ethics that it is the only theory we will consider here.

The early utilitarians, most notably Jeremy Bentham (1748–1832) – often thought of as the 'father' of utilitarianism – and John Stuart Mill (1806–73), were responding to a social environment in which the rise of secularism and atheism had left something of an intellectual vacuum. If God does not define for us what is right and wrong, they asked themselves, then how shall we know what to do? Influenced also by the rise of modern science, Bentham found what he believed to be the answer in

The 'Auto-Icon' of Jeremy Bentham at University College London. In his will Bentham directed that his body should be dissected for scientific research, and his skeleton be preserved and 'clad in one of the suits of black occasionally worn by me'.

the 'two sovereign masters' that all of us are subject to, namely pain and pleasure. The utilitarians reasoned that if pain is bad and pleasure is good then the clearest answer to the question 'what should we do' is to do that which minimises pain and maximises pleasure for the greatest number of those who are affected by our actions. The best-known statement of utilitarianism is that it defines right actions by what results in 'the greatest happiness for the greatest number'. Expressed in neutral terms (because, after all, some people prefer to be unhappy!), the idea is to maximise *utility* (that is, whatever it is that each individual needs/wants/ desires/prefers) for the greatest number.

As simple as this all sounds, there are a number of challenging questions within utilitarianism, and as a result there are different kinds of utilitarianism espoused by groups of thinkers who give different answers to those questions. When considering a group of people affected by some possible action, should we be interested in maximising the *overall amount* of utility in the group (in which case it is not a problem if the act makes some people very happy, and most people not much happier, or even a bit unhappy), or should we be interested in maximising utility for *each person* affected by the action? Should we weigh all forms of utility equally? (Bentham thought so, but Mill thought we should give more weight to what he called 'higher pleasures'.) Do we have to weigh up all the potential consequences for every decision we make, or are there some rules we can follow that will generally lead to utility maximising outcomes? (Those who think there are such rules are called 'rule utilitarians'.)

The two great strengths of utilitarianism are, firstly, that it takes consequences seriously, something that most of us find intuitively appealing; and, secondly, that (Mill aside) it is essentially neutral about what sorts of things matter, or are important – all that matters is whether or not they have utility for people. So in that respect it seems to maximise freedom of choice and equality of choice – it doesn't matter whether it is listening to opera or collecting toothpicks that gives you utility, it's that it gives you utility that matters.

That's not to say that utilitarianism doesn't face some serious challenges. In a way, the strongest objections to utilitarianism are the flip side of its greatest strengths. While most people intuitively agree that consequences matter in ethics, the exclusive focus on overall consequences in utilitarianism and other forms

The Colosseum in Rome. An example that is sometimes used to illustrate one of the challenges that utilitarianism faces is the case of the gladiators who fought and died here for the entertainment of Roman citizens. If the pleasure that the audiences gained from watching these gladiatorial contests was sufficient to outweigh the suffering of the gladiators themselves, then it seems difficult for utilitarians to say what was wrong with this practice.

of consequentialism (more about those below) seems to overlook the moral importance of the individual. If, say, the act that will maximise utility for most of the people affected involves harming or disrespecting an individual, there seems to be nothing in utilitarianism that would suggest we should hesitate to endorse that act. Likewise, many have objected that the focus on good consequences can override considerations of justice. The idea that 'the ends justify the means' is one that sits uncomfortably for many of us. Indeed, this kind of concern led Karl Popper (1902–94), one of the greatest philosophers of the 20th century, to state that 'it is not only impossible but very dangerous to attempt to maximize the pleasure or the happiness of the people, since such an attempt must lead to totalitarianism' (Popper 2002, 339). (Popper did not propose abandoning utilitarianism, but instead advocated for what he called 'negative utilitarianism', which replaces the goal of maximising pleasure with minimising pain.)

The focus on consequences also, in most forms of utilitarianism, largely treats motives as irrelevant – it's outcomes that matter, not intentions. But most of us would agree that it does matter, ethically, what our motives and intentions are in doing what we do. Consequences are, furthermore, often difficult to predict in advance, particularly when self-interest is involved (which is more often than not the case in ethics), which makes basing our ethical decisions entirely on our projections of future outcomes seem somewhat iffy. A related problem is that overall utility is difficult to calculate. Bentham was enthusiastic about the potential of reducing utilitarianism to a kind of scientific calculation, measuring 'utils' and 'hedons' in terms of such considerations as intensity, duration, certainty and remoteness. Most other utilitarians, however, have distanced themselves from this sort of thinking, and acknowledge that there's an inherent difficulty in trying to weigh up different, and sometimes incommensurable, goods. How, for example, are we to weigh the utility of a chocolate bar against the utility of a beautiful sunset?

Another set of challenges that utilitarianism faces centres on the neutrality of utility. As we've seen, even Mill was uncomfortable with this – do we *really* want to say that collecting toothpicks is as valuable and meaningful an activity as enjoying a great opera? If (as is undoubtedly the case) more people get more pleasure overall from watching television dramas than those who gain satisfaction from studying ancient manuscripts, are we really going to say that the money that is spent on preserving and protecting ancient manuscripts should be reallocated to television drama production?

Another challenge faced by utilitarianism is that it is extremely demanding. Often people think they are applying utilitarian thinking when they choose actions that lead to the best consequences for themselves and those they care about. But this is not utilitarianism at all, it is a largely discredited form of consequentialism known as 'ethical egoism' (discredited because it relies on the dubious claim that if we each seek our own happiness and ignore questions about the happiness or well-being of others, things will generally turn out for the best for everyone). The true utilitarian knows that when she weighs up courses of action her own happiness or utility, and that of those she cares about, should weigh no more than the happiness or utility of every other person affected, even complete strangers or enemies.

Despite these challenges and its comparatively short history utilitarianism is today arguably the most influential single approach to applied ethics.

References and further reading

Simon Blackburn. 2009. *Ethics: A Very Short Introduction*. Oxford University Press.

Karl Popper. 2002. *The Open Society and Its Enemies: Volume 2.* Routledge.

Russ Shafer-Landau. 2014. *The Fundamentals of Ethics*. Oxford University Press.

William H. Shaw. 2015. *Utilitarianism and the Ethics of War*. Routledge.

DEONTOLOGICAL ETHICS

PAULA KEATING

The most influential alternative to consequentialist theories of ethics is the deontological approach. The broad field of deontological ethics is made up of numerous ethical frameworks that have in common a foundational structural feature, namely that ethical behaviour is defined in terms of adherence to a set of ethical rules or duties. Examples of deontological ethical frameworks can be found throughout recorded human history – a well-known example is the Ten Commandments, found in the Hebrew Scriptures, which have a central place in Jewish and Christian ethics. While many deontological codes of ethics are religious in nature, there are also many that are not. Arguably the most influential theory of deontological ethics that is not dependent on a religious metaphysical underpinning is the ethical theory proposed by Immanuel Kant (1724–1804).

The problem Kant addresses in his moral philosophy can be summed up by his own question: what should I do? This is, of course, our problem too. The shortest answer we could say Kant gives to this question is, act morally! Before Kant, moral philosophy had many definitions of what it means to act morally. It had already been proposed that acting morally meant following the natural order of things, the social order, the will of God, moral feeling or the desire for happiness. Kant argues that if we follow these paths the demands of ethics or the demand to be good cannot be given objective validity. These previous conceptions of morals always come to be dependent on some condition or experience. For Kant the deontologist, if the command to act morally is to be at all useful it needs to be able to stand as an unconditional and universally reliable principle that is applicable across time and circumstance.

In order to find this objectively valid origin for moral philosophy, Kant begins with its subject – us! In particular, he begins with the phenomenon that we can and do act against what nature sets out before us. We can do things that don't make us happy, that we don't feel like doing, that aren't part of our repertoire of instincts, needs, desires and passions. We humans can choose to act against all of these strong conditions. For Kant, this is a very important point about being human. We have the ability to choose how we act because we have a capacity to will what we do. The will is an aspect of our faculty of reason that Kant called practical reason. Practical reason is the phenomenon that we don't just follow the laws of nature but rather can set our own laws, recognise them as principles and then direct our behaviour in accordance with them. Practical reason is nothing other than the will.

The will is what, in Kant's view, distinguishes humans from animals, who he argues are slaves to their own instincts. As humans, our practical reason (our will) is free from the laws of nature, it is autonomous because through the will we can decide on our own laws to follow. So, for example, even if I am hungry I can still choose to share the food I have with my brother. Kant grounds his practical reason – or ethics – on the idea of rational freedom, which is of course a much more involved concept for

Kant than the one just stated. Nonetheless enough has been said to explain what it means for Kant when he says 'Act!' It means use your practical reason, be a rational autonomous agent, use your will to write your own laws and follow them.

Understanding what 'act' means for Kant is important because all versions of his Categorical Imperative, one of the most famous ethical formulations in history, begin with this very word. Kant offered at least three formulations of the Categorical Imperative – some scholars would argue that there are five – but the versions of the Categorical Imperative that are most commonly employed by applied ethicists are:

> *The first formulation*: Act only in accordance with that maxim [or principle] through which you can at the same time will that it become a universal law.

> *The second formulation*: Act in such a way that you treat humanity, whether in your own person or in the person of any other, never merely as a means to an end, but always at the same time as an end.

The first formulation of the Categorical Imperative calls us to ensure that our reasons for acting are universal, that they are what everyone else in like circumstances ought to do. In order to be moral, Kant argues, we must put aside all our own wants and preferences, and determine our will as if we were legislating for all other wills in the world. The Categorical Imperative is the highest standard for all ethical behaviour. So, you ask yourself, am I acting with an intention that I also would want everyone else to have as their reason for acting? The Categorical Imperative commands us to not think of ourselves as just acting in isolation, but rather shows how our individual moral decisions are of general significance and concern the world at large.

The second formulation of the Categorical Imperative (Kant claimed that all of the different formulations amount to the same thing, though that is somewhat difficult to grasp) emphasises Kant's view that what matters most about human beings is that we can freely will (this idea is sometimes captured in the notion that we are *agents*). If that is what matters most about human beings, then our highest ethical duty to one another is to respect that fact, by not acting in a way that undermines other people's ability to exercise their practical reason (will). To treat them in such a way amounts to treating them as a mere means to an end, rather than respecting them as an agent. In our everyday language we capture what is problematic about such behaviour in phrases like 'You shouldn't use her that way' or 'You're just using me to get what you want!' Of course we do often use one another as a means to an end – if I ask you to make me a cup of coffee, then I am using you as a means to achieve my goal of enjoying a hot brew. But it is important not to overlook the phrase 'merely as a means' in Kant's second formulation of the Categorical Imperative. So long as you willingly *choose* to carry out my request to make me a cup of coffee – that is, so long as you exercise your will – then I have not used you as a *mere* means to my end. To use someone as a mere means to achieving my end means that we somehow bypass or override their ability to act on their free will. So, to continue with the example, if I point a gun at you and demand that you make me a cup of coffee, then I don't allow you to choose your course of action. Likewise, if I lie to you in order to get you to make me a cup of coffee (perhaps I say that the coffee is for someone else), then by not giving you the true facts of the situation I have voided your ability to freely choose what you wish to do. I have failed to *respect* you as a rational being.

Systems of deontological ethics face the criticism that they lack flexibility, and seem to ignore consequences despite the fact that consequences clearly seem to matter in ethics. Kant's ethics faces this criticism in the form of the 'inquiring murderer' case. It seems that if someone intent on committing murder were to ask a good Kantian to reveal the location of the murderer's intended prey, the Kantian would – as directed by the categorical imperative – be required to tell the truth to the murderer. This is clearly problematic! Another criticism of deontological ethics in general is that sometimes circumstances arise in which two or more ethical principles seem to apply, but in a manner that offers conflicting direction about what the right thing to do is. A delightful hypothetical example of this, set in the context of a cricket match, is raised in Colin Radford's classic short paper 'The Umpire's Dilemma' (1985).

References and further reading

Manfred Kuehn. 2001. *Kant: A Biography*. Cambridge University Press.

Brian Orend. 2000. *War and International Justice: An International Perspective*. Wilfrid Laurier University Press.

Thomas W. Pogge. 1988. 'The Categorical Imperative', in *Kant's Groundwork of the Metaphysics of Morals*, ed. Paul Guyer. Rowman & Littlefield.

Colin Radford. 1985. 'The Umpire's Dilemma'. *Analysis* 45 (2), pp. 109–11.

John Rawls. 2000. 'Kant', in *Lectures on the History of Moral Philosophy*, ed. Barbara Hermann. Harvard University Press.

VIRTUE ETHICS

TOM FRAME

Implicit in the ancient writings of Plato (428/427 or 424/423–348/347 BC) and more particularly Aristotle (384–322 BC), 'virtue ethics' is one of the oldest approaches to normative ethics still studied by modern philosophers. Virtue ethics is distinguished from other major theories in its emphasis on virtues or moral character ahead of the 'deontological' approach, which highlights duties and rules, and 'consequentialism', which concentrates on outcomes. The primary or cardinal virtues canvassed in Plato's *Republic* are prudence, justice, fortitude and temperance. They are a form of knowledge and are necessary for the acquisition of ultimate goodness. In Aristotle's *Nicomachean Ethics* produced in the fourth century BC, the goal of human striving is not power, wealth or prestige but the exercise of rationality in accordance with the virtues so as to produce traits like honesty, friendliness and pride.

In focusing on personal traits rather than individual actions, virtue ethics transcends the question of whether an action is good or bad. Instead, it offers guidance on the whole of a person's life, with special interest in the kinds of aptitudes and attributes a good person should seek to acquire and display. Virtue ethics is not, therefore, primarily interested in what an individual might

A view of the Acropolis in Athens, Greece. Ancient Greece was the birthplace of Western philosophy, and it was in Athens that Aristotle lived and taught his philosophy of virtue.

do but in what they might become, as a means of building a more moral society that essentially encourages virtues more than it discourages vice.

Virtue ethics was the preferred approach in Western moral philosophy until the Enlightenment, influencing both Christian and non-Christian thinkers. It regained Anglo-American prominence with the article 'Modern Moral Philosophy' by the British analytical philosopher G.E.M. Anscombe (1919–2001), which reflected prevailing dissatisfaction with contemporary deontology and utilitarianism when first published in 1958. Her thinking, particularly in her seminal work *Intention*, was complemented by the work of Sir Bernard Williams (1929–2003) on truth and truthfulness and the claim by Alasdair MacIntyre in

After Virtue? that moral communities are crucial to the formation of virtuous individuals. Each philosopher called for a change of emphasis in moral philosophy from rules and obligations to practices and habits that have the potential to generate virtues and enrich social interactions.

There are three main strands of modern virtue ethics. The first strand is classical 'Eudaimonism', which discloses its continuing debt to Greek philosophy in three related concepts: *arête* (the virtues); *phronesis* (practical wisdom); and *eudaimonia* (flourishing). The virtues are essentially habits that allow individuals to succeed in their appointed purpose. By practising the virtues in the course of everyday life, a person will achieve *eudaimonia* – which can be translated as 'the good life' or as 'well-being'. Instead of fixating on whether a particular action is right or wrong, or good or bad, Eudaimonism poses the more expansive question: 'how should I live?' For Aristotle, the distinctive functioning of human beings is reasoning. Therefore, a good life is a consistently reasoned one.

The second strand emphasises the importance of agency and is associated with the contemporary American philosopher Michael Slote, who contends that virtues are those characteristics, such as compassion, kindness and generosity, we identify and find admirable in the lives of other people – our moral exemplars. Evaluating actions depends on the ethical quality of the inner life of those who perform them.

The ethics of care, the third strand, has been promoted mainly by feminist philosophers, such as the New Zealand-born Annette Baier (1929–2012), who have argued that familiar feminine traits, such as caring and nurturing, which are essential for human wholeness and social happiness, have been neglected by men who think of virtues in masculine terms, leading them to elevate autonomy and justice to pre-eminence.

The three strands of virtue ethics are united in their commitment to the following general principles.

- In order to live well a person needs moral characteristics called virtues.
- A virtuous person is one who acts virtuously at all times.
- A person acts virtuously if and when they possess and exercise the virtues.
- An action is only right if it is an action that a virtuous person would carry out in similar circumstances.

Significantly, most virtue theorists insist that for an action to be declared virtuous it must be the outcome of a rational decision and not the product of instinct. Being virtuous requires thought and demands choices.

Like any approach, virtue ethics has its strengths and weaknesses. It tends to offer generalised advice rather than provide specific counsel. While its emphasis on the totality of the human person works against compartmentalising the ethical aspects of human interaction from a person's economic or political outlook, it does not provide clear guidance, for instance, on resolving moral dilemmas in which the choice is not between good and bad but the lesser of two evils where one is obliged to select from equally unpalatable options. Critics of virtue ethics have also questioned the inventory of virtues provided by its proponents, asking why some virtues deserve to be more esteemed than others and arguing that agendas far removed from moral philosophy may be exerting an unexamined influence. For instance, cultural preferences and prejudices may be the basis upon which certain behaviours are subjectively elevated to prominence rather than on their intrinsic value or collective worth. Others think the whole approach unfair as some people will be fortunate and receive sound moral nurture, while others will be exposed to appalling examples of immorality through no fault of their own.

Although virtue ethics has a formidable pedigree claiming many profound thinkers of considerable erudition, it remains the minority approach, particularly in the field of applied ethics, which has been dominated by the deontological–utilitarian debate. In recent years an increasing number of virtue ethicists have written on issues in applied ethics, while some have attempted to move from moral philosophy to political philosophy in which virtue ethics addresses questions of statecraft and nationhood. The continuing emphasis on the training of character in virtue ethics remains its most significant contribution to modern Western life.

References and further reading

G.E.M. Anscombe. 1958. 'Modern Moral Philosophy'. *Philosophy* 33 (124), pp. 1–19.

G.E.M. Anscombe. 2000. *Intention.* Second edition, Harvard University Press.

Roger Crisp and Michael Slote (eds). 1997. *Virtue Ethics.* Oxford University Press.

Rosalind Hursthouse. 1999. *On Virtue Ethics.* Oxford University Press.

Alasdair MacIntyre. 2007. *After Virtue: A Study in Moral Theory.* Third edition, University of Notre Dame Press.

Daniel C. Russell (ed.). 2013. *The Cambridge Companion to Virtue Ethics.* Cambridge University Press.

5

STOICISM AND THE PROFESSION OF ARMS

RICHARD ADAMS

Stoicism is a virtue ethic that is well expressed by the adage 'bear and forebear', (Epictetus 1998, 10.5–8). Stoicism resonates strongly with the fabled military traits of self-control, discipline and endurance. Thus, while Stoicism is a minority view in contemporary ethics in general, the particular appeal of this philosophy to military personnel makes it a pertinent topic for this book.

Stoicism was made famous as a philosophy for the profession of arms by Vice Admiral James Bond Stockdale, USN (1923–2005). A naval aviator, Stockdale was shot down in 1965 and captured by the North Vietnamese. Enduring over seven years in the notorious prison known as the 'Hanoi Hilton', Stockdale was in solitary confinement for four years, in leg irons for two years and tortured fifteen times. In 1976 he was awarded the Medal of Honor for indefatigable resistance as a prisoner of war. Famously it was the writings of the Stoic Epictetus which inspired Stockdale in his gallant defiance.

In Epictetus, Stockdale found a hard-edged philosophy which

Statue of Vice Admiral James Bond Stockdale outside Luce Hall at the United States Naval Academy, Annapolis, Maryland. Luce Hall is home to the Naval Academy's Stockdale Center for Ethical Leadership as well as the Department of Leadership, Ethics and Law.

will 'do you good if your child dies, or if your brother dies, or if you must die or be tortured... (if you must be) enchained, how to be racked, how to be exiled' (Stockdale 1993, 5). Stockdale described Stoicism as the proper philosophy for the military arts (Stockdale 1995, 21; 1993, 3, 6).

A forerunner of Stoic thought was Socrates, who epitomised

Stoic indifference to physical comfort and showed himself to be devoid of pretence. When unjustly put on trial for his life, Socrates''refusal to escape, his calmness in the face of death, and his conviction that the perpetrator of injustice injures himself more than his victim, all fitted in perfectly with stoic teaching' (Russell 1995, 261), according to which the tribulations of every-day life are held to have no real power to affect human attitudes. Stoicism also strongly reflects Socrates' view that it is only the good will that truly matters.

From the philosophy known as Cynicism came the idea that the 'nature or *physis* of a man consists in his rationality' (Long 1974, 110). Investing this principle with particular stringency, the Cynics argued that people need nothing apart from physical and mental self-discipline. Thus, the so-called 'externals' – things conventionally regarded as good such as property and reputa-tion – are irrelevant to human flourishing. Likewise focused on self-mastery, the Stoic dismisses possessions, offices and honours as things that delude us and draw us away from what truly matters, *prohairesis* – which we might understand as moral char-acter, integrity, will or self. Likewise, the Stoic sees fear, concern and anxieties as insubstantial pretenders which, properly under-stood, are insufficient to impede us in fulfilling our moral duty. For the Stoic, self-respect – *aidos* – is a decisive moral quality. Thus, the philosophy belittles physical harm, since physical harm is nothing in comparison to the devastating agony of shame should a person fall down in a duty.

As Stockdale's example shows, Stoicism is a potentially powerful worldview for military personnel. Nonetheless, as a general philosophy of life Stoicism faces the criticism that it undermines our humanity, particularly in assigning the rela-tionships that most of us take as central to human flourishing – including those with our families, friends and colleagues – to the pile of 'externals' to which we are expected to be indifferent. For military personnel there are two further particular points of concern. The first is the possibility that Stoic idealism contributes to post-traumatic stress. The second is the possibility that Stoic soldiers, fulfilling their duty as they see it, become implicated in crimes of obedience.

Resilient and dependable, the Stoic is a soldier of substance and obligation. But the sense of commitment and duty, characteristic of the philosophy, sows the seed of vulnerability. This is because Stoicism is not a defence against the betrayal of 'what's right' by the institutions – political and military – in which soldiers trust. Furthermore, conditioned as they are to obey without question, and resolved to do their duty without flinching, Stoic soldiers may commit what has been called 'crimes of obedience' – those atrocities which occur when authorities give orders that exceed the bounds of morality or law. The moral injury or damage which follows from the betrayal of 'what's right' is recognised by Jonathan Shay in his book, *Achilles in Vietnam* (1995). Shay acknowledges the post-traumatic stress which follows inexorably from terror, shock and grief at the death of friends. But veterans, he argues, may be expected to recover from horror, fear and grief. Far less certain is recovery from the moral injury which follows from violation of the soldier's sense of rightness.

Accordingly, the obligations of Stoicism may be seen as extending beyond the obligations of the individual soldier. Stoicism imposes obligations on the military institution to safeguard the mental well-being of the soldiers who serve. Expecting soldiers to bear the burden of their duty stoically, the military leadership bears a reciprocal onus to preserve a sense of 'what's right', to preserve the moral value of words and to respect moral ideals as being of more than propaganda value.

References and further reading

Epictetus. 1998. *Fragments*, in W.A. Oldfather (tr.), (1998) *Discourses, Fragments, The Encheiridion* (two volumes). Harvard University Press.

Anthony Arthur Long. 1974. *Hellenistic Philosophy.* Charles Scribner's Sons.

Bertrand Russell. 1995. *The History of Western Philosophy.* Routledge.

Jonathan Shay. 1995. *Achilles in Vietnam: Combat Trauma and the Undoing of Character.* Simon & Schuster.

James Bond Stockdale. 1993. *Courage Under Fire: Testing Epictetus's Doctrines in a Laboratory of Human Behavior (Hoover Essays).* Hoover Institution Press.

James Bond Stockdale. 1995. *Thoughts of a Philosophical Fighter Pilot.* Hoover Institution Press.

ETHICAL
TRIANGULATION

DEANE-PETER BAKER

As the other chapters in this section make clear, there are essentially three distinct fundamental approaches to ethics. One approach focuses on ensuring good consequences (consequentialism), another focuses on following ethical rules or principles that are mostly intended to ensure respect for others (deontology), and the third approach takes good character, or virtue, as the central feature of the ethical life (virtue ethics). For most of us, each of these approaches resonates deeply. The idea that consequences matter in ethics has strong intuitive appeal, as does the notion that others are deserving of our respect and should not be treated merely as a means to an end. Likewise, there are few of us who don't feel the pull of character-based concepts like courage, integrity, compassion and honour.

We have also seen, however, that each of these approaches faces challenges. Utilitarianism, the dominant form of consequentialism, seems to have trouble accounting for the importance of the individual, and sometimes seems to give rise to counter-intuitive results. Likewise, deontological theories of ethics, such as that developed by Immanuel Kant, can sometimes seem too rigid and blind to the importance of consequences in certain circumstances.

Stoicism (a virtue theory) represents an enormously powerful way to face conditions of hardship, but that seems to come at the cost of some aspects of our humanity. More generally, virtue approaches to ethics, with their focus on what we should *be*, don't seem to offer us enough clear guidance about what we should *do* when dealing with moral dilemmas. (This is by no means a comprehensive account of the challenges faced by each of these approaches to ethics; please see the previous chapters for more detail.)

That leaves us with a problem to solve. If we're really interested in taking on ethical challenges with more than just our gut reactions, and we see both the pros and cons of these three broad approaches to ethics, then how should we proceed? One answer is to choose the approach to ethics that seems most correct and dig deeper into the literature to find ways in which that approach can be refined in order to minimise or negate the challenges we have discussed, as well as others we haven't mentioned. If you do that you will find that there is a deep and immensely rich tradition of thought associated with each of these three approaches that has been built up over time by some of the finest philosophical minds our world has ever seen. (The 'References and further reading' sections of the preceding chapters will give you a good starting point if you want to start digging.) We might call this the *philosophical approach*.

The other approach to this problem is what we might call the *pragmatic approach*. Here, rather than try to resolve the philosophical difficulties inherent in any of these broad approaches to ethics, we instead apply a practical methodology that seeks to (as far as is possible) get the best out of all three approaches while avoiding their worst pitfalls. This is, in practice, what many well-trained applied ethicists do – apply each of the different approaches and concepts as they best fit the circumstances concerned.

A weathervane, indicating the points of the compass, at a former Second World War Royal Air Force airfield in Lancashire, England. Navigation through physical space offers a useful analogy for the process of working through ethical challenges, both in the military and in general.

What makes this *pragmatic approach* work for professional ethicists is their deep and intuitive understanding of the theory. For most non-specialists, however, there is value in having an explicit methodology to guide us. This chapter outlines one such approach, one I have developed over years of teaching ethics to military officers in training, first at the United States Naval Academy and now at the Australian Defence Force Academy.

I call this approach Ethical Triangulation. The idea of 'triangulation' resonates with military personnel because of the importance of navigation in the military, and the idea fits well with the tripartite nature of mainstream ethical theory. In its simplest form the idea is to, as it were, 'take a bearing' from each of the main approaches to ethics when considering an ethically challenging question. This ensures that we don't overlook any important ethical considerations that might be obscured by applying only one ethical approach, and also benefits from the fact that the strengths of each of these approaches often fall in exactly the ethical 'space' that the weaknesses of one or both of the other approaches are.

As an explicit methodology Ethical Trangulation works like this. The first step is to take a bearing from the ethical peak of 'Respect' (deontology), by asking ourselves what ethical principles or rules apply to the situation we are considering. For some this is a little counter-intuitive as, in my experience, many of us want to begin by examining potential consequences. But there are good reasons for starting with deontology rather than consequentialism. For one thing, deontological theories of ethics represent what we might think of as the collected ethical wisdom of the ages, and the principles embedded in deontological ethics are often (as rule utilitarians recognise) a good guide to achieving the best consequences. Add that to one of the key limitations of consequentialism – that we're often poor at predicting consequences, particularly when self-interest is involved – and you have good reason to start with deontology.

Once we have identified the deontological principles that apply to the case in question, we will either have a first suggestion of what the ethically appropriate action or actions should be, or else we will find that there are competing principles that suggest different courses of action. The next step is to look to the horizon again and consider the possible consequences of the course or courses of action that we are weighing up. In so doing, we might find that the potential consequences of the course of action suggested by our assessment of the deontological principles are serious enough, and certain enough, that those consequences outweigh the deontological principles. This will then point us to a different ethical solution. Alternatively we might find that weighing up the consequences favours one course of action over the alternatives in those cases where conflicting deontological principles suggest different ways forward.

The third step is to take a final bearing from the ethical peak of 'Character' (virtue ethics). This step shifts our attention, for a moment, away from the issue under consideration onto ourselves and what we know about ourselves. This will, of course, be meaningless if we do not know our character well, and here it is worth reminding ourselves of one of the most famous quotes in all of philosophy, alleged to have been uttered by Socrates, that 'the unexamined life is not worth living' (Plato 1966, 38a). In this step we ask ourselves whether the course of action that our reflection thus far has led us to favour is what a virtuous person would do (an act that is courageous, compassionate, impartial, honourable, and so on), or whether our thinking has been influenced by some or other character flaws (vices) that we know ourselves to possess, such as laziness, selfishness or rashness. Just as a strong magnet can throw off the needle of a compass, our vices can, if we are not careful, affect our ethical decision-making and point us in the wrong ethical direction.

Deliberately working through these three steps of Ethical Triangulation should help us, in general, to make better ethical judgments than we would otherwise, and in many cases – perhaps even most – that will be all that is needed. Ethics is not, however, a perfect science, and while this process will certainly help us to exclude a significant number of possible courses of action as clearly inappropriate, it is possible that sometimes there will still be an unresolved conflict between two or more possible options that could perhaps be the right thing to do. Here we reach again for the resources of virtue theory, in particular the notion of *phroesis* or practical wisdom. In this grey area in which theory-driven analysis is sometimes inadequate to the task of giving us final guidance, it becomes a matter of wisdom of how to proceed. Practical wisdom is the ability to appropriately marry up right intentions and good character with practical action. It is the product of experience and the practice of virtuous living, and we will often do well in such cases to seek out guidance from those wiser than ourselves. Some will find this lack of analytic precision in such cases to be frustrating, but we would do well to remember the wisdom of Aristotle himself, who reminds us that 'It is the mark of an educated man to look for precision in each class of things just so far as the nature of the subject admits; it is evidently equally foolish to accept probable reasoning from a mathematician and to demand from a rhetorician scientific proofs' (Aristotle 1984, Book I, 1094.b24).

References and further reading

Aristotle (1984). Nichomachean Ethics, in *The Complete Works of Aristotle: The Revised Oxford Translation*. Jonathan Barnes (ed). Princeton University Press.

Jules Evans (2013). *Philosophy for Life and Other Dangerous Situations*. New World Library.

Rita Manning and Scott R. Stroud (2008). *A Practical Guide to Ethics: Living and Leading with Integrity*. Westview Press.

Plato (1966). *Plato in Twelve Volumes, Vol. 1.* Translated by Harold North Fowler. Harvard University Press.

PART TWO
STATE AUTHORITY, SOCIETY AND THE MILITARY

The Arc de Triomphe, a symbol of state authority and military power.

THE SOCIAL CONTRACT

PETER BALINT

Let's assume you serve in the military. Your superiors tell you what to wear, where to go, which activities you must do, and which ones you are forbidden from undertaking. If you don't comply with these orders, you can either be forced or punished – both of which are backed by coercive force. Why is this legitimate? And how is it any different from being kidnapped by terrorists who wish to play soldiers?

One answer (assuming you are not a conscript) is that you actively *consented* to this relationship (see Chapter 12: Role morality and the unlimited liability contract). In most modern militaries, you will have both literally 'signed up', as well as sworn a public oath of allegiance. The power that is wielded against you is legitimate because you agreed to it. This agreement even includes occasions when you disagree with what you are being asked to do. This isn't to say it's never okay to resist (see Chapter 16: Illegal orders and whistle-blowing), just that you can be legitimately forced to do something you don't want to do – and all because of your initial agreement.

You may wonder what all this has to do with *the social contract*. The question that political theorists have grappled with for centuries is, 'what makes political power legitimate?' Why is it okay for the state and those who serve it to tell you what to do, force you to pay taxes, and fine and even jail you for non-compliance? If any other group or institution tried to do this sort of thing we would think it outrageous and probably akin to a kind of slavery (in fact the political theorist Robert Nozick (1938–2002) famously argued that taxation levied by the state *is* a form of partial slavery (Nozick 1974), but as that's a minority view we'll set it aside here). What's so special then about our relationship to our own political community that can justify such force potentially being used against us?

One answer might be that emotion and identity tie us together. We feel national pride, feel connected with others who we have never met and who may live half a continent away, and identify that we are one 'people'. This is certainly true of many of us, particularly those who feel patriotic. But not all of us feel this tie, and many who do feel this tie of national identification still get quite upset when they are forced to do things they don't want to (such as pay taxes, drive to the speed limit, or report for jury duty). National identification does not fully explain the relationship.

A more practical answer might be that the state has all the power, and you'd be stupid not to follow their orders. This is true. Disobeying orders from your state or its agents is pretty dangerous. But if it's just a matter of holding the guns, then our state starts to look very similar to a bunch of thugs. If somebody pulls a gun on you, you're going to do what they say. It would be good if there's more to state power than this.

The most famous answer to this question of legitimate political power is the one given by Thomas Hobbes, John Locke and Jean-Jacques Rousseau: consent. That is, we have somehow agreed to have this power wielded over us. Importantly, unlike the military case, the agreement is not between us and our states, but between us and our fellow citizens; our political community. This is what makes it a *social* contract. The contract ties us to our fellow citizens and makes us subject to the form and content of the political community's collective decision-making. The contract gives us a special relationship with our fellow citizens, and provides a reason why we may owe more to our fellow citizens than distant foreigners (something that is hard to justify if the moral equality of individuals is accepted). So the reason the state can tell us what to do and the reason we have a special relationship with our fellow citizens is because we said, 'Yes I agree to be in this relationship'.

The White House Peace Vigil, an anti-nuclear peace vigil outside the White House in Washington, D.C. According to social contract theory governments gain their authority through a tacit or hypothetical contract in which citizens agree with one another to submit to the rule of the state in exchange for the security the state provides.

At this point, many of you might be thinking 'I never agreed to this! When did I sign up? Where's my contract?' And this is a big problem. It is true that most of us, at least those born in the country we now live in, never did give *express consent* to anything at all. That doesn't apply to everyone, though. Anyone who has gone through a citizenship ceremony – that is, migrants – certainly has expressly consented.

But for the majority of the population who were born in the country where they now reside, the problem remains. Social contract theorists try to show two other ways in which we can be said to have consented. The first is that while we may not have sworn allegiance or signed a contract, we've done lots of things that show we agree with this relationship. We've driven on the roads, voted in elections, and perhaps just not moved to another country. We have demonstrated *tacit consent*.

The problem here is that for consent to be legitimate, it must be intentional. Otherwise, you could unwittingly consent to all sorts of things. For consent to be valid, we need for it to be clear which actions demonstrate consent and what is actually being consented to – something that cannot be said driving on roads or voting in elections etc.

It also matters that the consent is voluntary. When a mugger holding a gun says, 'Give me your phone and wallet or I'll shoot you', it would be strange to say you have consented to giving these items away. Most of us would think you didn't really have a choice. (The political theorist Thomas Hobbes (1588–1679) is the exception here – for him, 'your money or your life' is a free choice!) Likewise, what choice does someone born and raised in a particular country have to leave it, or at least not without some very high costs?

The second strategy used by social contract theorists to demonstrate consent by all of the population is *hypothetical*.

The argument here is that once we realise how bad life would be living outside of the state – in Hobbes' famous words 'nasty, brutish, and short' – then it would be entirely rational for us to consent. Perhaps it would be rational, but the idea of hypothetical consent is controversial. As the American political theorist Ronald Dworkin (1931–2013) put, it: 'A hypothetical contract is not merely a pale form of an actual contract; it is no contract at all' (Dworkin 1997, 186).

Despite these problems with using the social contract to legitimise state power, the idea that we've somehow agreed remains the most popular explanation of why we're tied to our fellow citizens, and why it's okay that the state can force us to do things. The social contract is also a significant part of what explains the state's right to use force against others – that is, a state's right to raise and employ military forces. Under the social contract we agree to allow the state to take over, and exercise on our behalf, our basic rights to defend ourselves, our property and one another. To do that the state needs the means to not only protect us from one another (which is what the police and legal system are for) but also from outside attackers. So in an important sense a good part of the justification for the existence of the military can be said to come from the social contract.

References and further reading

Ronald Dworkin. 1997. *Taking Rights Seriously*. Bloomsbury.

Christopher W. Morris (ed.). 2000. *The Social Contract Theorists: Critical Essays on Hobbes, Locke and Rousseau*. Rowman & Littlefield.

Robert Nozick. 1974. *Anarchy, State and Utopia*. Basic Books.

Brian Skyrms. 2014. *The Evolution of the Social Contract*. Second edition, Cambridge University Press.

CIVIL-MILITARY RELATIONS

DEANE-PETER BAKER

There are essentially two ways to understand the concept of civil–military relations, one broad, and one narrow. The broad interpretation of civil–military relations is that it describes the relationship between the military and civilian society in general. The narrow interpretation of the term focuses on the relationship between the military and the civil authority (government) of the society in question. While much of the research related to this issue focuses on empirical questions, this chapter will briefly discuss the central ethical questions related to civil–military relations.

In terms of the broad interpretation of civil–military relations, a key concept is the idea of the 'civil–military gap'. This is the notion that because of the unique role and norms of the military profession, there exists an inevitable separation between the military and the society it serves. As Richard Kohn points out, 'The military is, by necessity, among the least democratic institutions in human experience; martial customs and procedures clash by nature with individual freedom and civil liberty, the highest values in democratic societies' (Kohn 1997, 141). In one sense this gap seems not only inevitable, but necessary – an excessively 'civilianised' military would, many scholars argue, result in an ineffectual military, which would represent a failure of the military to play its role as mandated by the social contract (see Chapter 7). On the other hand, if the civil–military gap grows too wide there is a danger that the military will lose sight of its role as a servant of society at large, and will instead seek to become society's master. When this happens, military *coups d'etat* can occur, often with tragic results. Military dictatorships are, with few exceptions, associated with oppression and human rights abuses.

Keeping the civil–military gap from growing too large is, therefore, ethically important. One positive factor in this regard is a society that appropriately recognises and honours its military servants through such things as national rituals (such as public

Londres 38 (38 London Street) in Santiago, Chile, where opponents of the military junta led by General Augusto Pinochet (1915–2006) were detained, tortured and murdered. It is a reminder of what can happen when a state's military fails to submit to democratic control.

holidays and events that recognise the honourable sacrifice of past and present members of the military), adequate provision of medical care and other benefits for serving and retired members of the military, and the like. Historically the practice of conscription (see Chapter 9) has been viewed as playing an important role in keeping society 'in touch' with the military. This practice has, however, largely fallen away in most liberal democracies, though a growing dependence on military reservists might perhaps compensate for this to some degree.

The narrower interpretation of civil–military relations (the issue of the relationship between the military and the civilian government) is sometimes described in terms of 'the democratic control of armed forces'. The assumption built into this terminology is that only democracy can ensure the kind of relationship between society and the state that is required by the social contract. The military, while playing an important role in advising the elected leadership, is expected to respond to civilian direction regardless of whether or not the military agrees with that direction. As Peter Feaver puts it, regarding military affairs, 'in a democracy, civilians have the right to be wrong' (Feaver 2003, 65). There are two aspects of the democratic control of armed force. There is, firstly, the question of ensuring that the elected government is accountable to the will of the electorate in its use of armed force. This is why in the United States only Congress has the power to declare war, and why many analysts argue that it is problematic that the President has the power to employ military force without a declaration of war.

The second aspect of this narrower interpretation of civil–military relations (the democratic control of armed forces) is the question of ensuring that the military remains subservient and responsive to the nation's elected civilian leadership. The two key academic figures who have addressed this question are Samuel P.

Huntington and Morris Janowitz in their landmark books *The Soldier and the State: The Theory and Politics of Civil–Military Relations* (Huntington 1957) and *The Professional Soldier: A Social and Political Portrait* (Janowitz 1960). Central to the theory of both Huntington and Janowitz is the concept of military professionalism. It is professionalism that ensures (in Huntington's terminology) 'objective civilian control', which involves:

1 a high level of military professionalism and recognition by military officers of the limits of their professional competence;

2 the effective subordination of the military to the civilian political leaders who make the basic decisions on foreign and military policy;

3 the recognition and acceptance by that leadership of an area of professional competence and autonomy for the military; and

4 as a result, the minimization of military intervention in politics and of political intervention in the military (Huntington 1995, 9–10).

Janowitz's analysis is more sociological than Huntington's, and the two approaches can be read as being largely complementary. The main area of difference between these two thinkers is that Huntington strongly advocated for a clear separation between the values of the military and those of the society they serve, which he believed to be essential for military effectiveness, while Janowitz argued that it is important that the values of the military reflect those of the society they serve.

More recently another important view of civil–military relations has arisen, Peter Feaver's 'Agency Theory'. While not disputing that military professionalism is an important factor in securing appropriate civil–military relations, Feaver points out that in practice states make use of a range of other tools to ensure military compliance. Basing his theory on 'principal–agent theory' (as employed in economics and other similar fields), Feaver starts with the observation that there exists an inescapable state of strategic tension between the preferences of the state's civilian leadership and those of the military. Using terminology borrowed from principal–agent theory, Feaver argues that the preference of the civilian leaders or principals is that the military 'work', while the preference of the military is to 'shirk'. 'Working', in this context, does not simply mean doing something but rather doing what matches the preferences of the civilian principals, while 'shirking' is failing to do so. Thus a military force can be very active, engaged in all sorts of projects and even wars, but still, in this sense, be shirking.

Feaver argues that civilian principals have available, and employ, a range of means to try to ensure that the military is working rather than shirking. These include forms of monitoring and punishment such as restricting the scope of delegation to the military; contractual incentives (relating to granting autonomy to the military within the scope of its areas of expertise); screening and selection mechanisms; 'fire alarms' (for example, think tanks and the media that report on the military); 'police patrols' (such as government investigations of the military); revocation of delegated authority; budget cuts and withdrawal of privileges; forced detachment from the military; military justice; and extra-legal civilian action.

An important aspect of Feaver's theory is that it describes means that are available to civilian principals to hold their state's military forces accountable where those forces do not have an established ethic of professionalism and subservience to the military, as is the case, for example, in new democracies or where states have disbanded and reformed their military forces. None of this, however, undermines the ethical imperative for military personnel to strive towards the kind of professionalism described by Huntington and Janowitz.

References and further reading

Deane-Peter Baker. 2007. 'Agency Theory: A New Model of Civil–Military Relations for Africa?' *African Journal of Conflict Resolution*, pp. 113–35.

Peter D. Feaver. 2003. *Armed Servants: Agency, Oversight, and Civil–Military Relations*. Harvard University Press.

Samuel P. Huntington. 1957. *The Soldier and the State: The Theory and Politics of Civil–Military Relations*. Harvard University Press.

Samuel P. Huntington. 1995. 'Reforming Civil–Military Relations'. *Journal of Democracy* 6 (4), pp. 9–17.

Morris Janowitz. 1960. *The Professional Soldier: A Social and Political Portrait*. Macmillan.

Richard H. Kohn. 1997. 'How Democracies Control the Military'. *Journal of Democracy* 8 (4), pp. 140–53.

CONSCRIPTION

DEANE-PETER BAKER

Conscription – also referred to variously as 'national service' or (in the United States) 'the draft' – is a form of mandatory service to the state, usually military service, which is imposed on citizens and which is legally enforced.

The modern practice of conscription dates back to the beginning of the 19th century, during the period of the French Revolution, when the new French Republic found itself under attack by Europe's monarchies. Unable to match the quality of the professional forces of France's opponents, Napoleon Bonaparte opted instead for quantity, conscripting millions of Frenchmen into his *Grande Armée* (Great Army) in what became known as the *levée en masse* (mass mobilisation). This massed military manpower gave Napoleon such an advantage that most major powers quickly followed suit and introduced conscription themselves. Conscription reached its apogee in the Second World War, with most of the major powers (though not the United States) employing conscription as a means to populate the massive armies needed to prosecute that conflict.

Today conscription is on the wane as quality has once again taken the ascendency and the greater sophistication of modern warfare increasingly demands a level of expertise and profession-

Portrait of Napoleon Bonaparte in the Palace of Versailles, France. Napoleon's institution of the *levée en masse* marked the beginning of modern conscription.

alism that is easier to achieve in an all-volunteer force. None-theless there remain important exceptions, such as Israel and Singapore, and many countries that no longer conscript their citizens into the military retain the legal right to do so should the government decide that circumstances make it necessary. In the first decade of the 21st century the United States controversially applied a policy known as 'stop loss' to tens of thousands of its troops. This policy forces volunteer military personnel to stay on active duty beyond the period of service defined in their employment contracts. Many critics saw stop loss as a form of 'backdoor' conscription, though this has been countered by those who point out that US servicemen and women accept the possibility that stop loss will be applied to them when they sign up for military service.

Those in favour of conscription argue that, apart from the military capability it brings (a subject of considerable debate), there are moral and social reasons why conscription should be in place. First, proponents argue, conscription satisfies a moral duty that rests on all citizens to play their part in ensuring the security of the state. Because all citizens benefit from the safety that an effective state military apparatus brings, all (so the argument goes) should be willing to play their part – and if necessary risk their lives – to contribute to the defence of the state and its interests. Furthermore, proponents contend, conscription plays an important role in *nation building*. Through mandatory military service individual citizens from different backgrounds are brought together and form a common identity through a shared commitment to serving their fellow citizens. It is also argued that, because conscript armies bring the military closer to society in general, states with conscript armies will be less likely to engage in risky, and perhaps unjustified, military ventures because conscript casualties will be felt more keenly in society than the deaths of volunteer professionals.

In response, critics point out that conscription fails to ensure that all citizens fulfil their moral duty to one another (even if it were accepted that such a duty includes the duty to risk one's life, which is controversial) because conscription is almost never applied fairly to all citizens. For one thing, with few exceptions, conscription is applied only to men. Furthermore, in practice, the

Singapore's iconic skyline. Singapore is one of the few developed countries to maintain universal military conscription.

burden of conscription falls more heavily onto lower economic classes, as the wealthy have the resources to enable them to 'work the system' to have their young men either avoid military service or be assigned to roles or units that ensured that they are unlikely to see combat. During the Vietnam War, for example, some units were given the informal title of 'Champagne units' because of the high proportion of young men from wealthy and well-connected families assigned to them.

The strongest argument against conscription is that it represents an illegitimate violation of the individual's right to liberty and, potentially, the individual's right to life. Furthermore, mandatory military service also violates the individual's right to act on his (or occasionally her) conscience. While many states that have practised or do practise conscription allow for waivers or alternative forms of service to be granted in the case of conscientious objectors who object in general to participating in war (this is usually, but not always, restricted to those whose pacifism rests on religious grounds), the right of conscripts to selective conscientious objection – in which the person concerned objects not to war in general but to the justice of the specific war or conflict which he or she is being called to participate in – is only recognised in law in one country in the world, Australia.

References and further reading

Tom Vanden Brook. 2008. 'More Forced to Stay in Service'. *USA Today* 23 April 2008. Accessed at http://usatoday30. usatoday.com/news/military/2008-04-21-stoploss_N.htm [accessed 19 March 2015].

Stephen Coleman and Nikki Coleman (with Richard Adams). 2014. 'Selective Conscientious Objection in Australia', in *When Soldiers Say No: Selective Conscientious Objection in the Modern Military* (Andrea Ellner, Paul Robinson and David Whetham, eds). Ashgate, pp. 99–114.

Michael L. Gross. 2005. 'Physician-Assisted Draft Evasion: Civil Disobedience, Medicine and War'. *Cambridge Quarterly of Healthcare Ethics* 14 (4), pp. 444–54.

Cheyne C. Ryan. 2004. 'Self Defence and the Obligations to Kill and Die'. *Ethics & International Affairs* 18 (1), pp. 69–73.

REPRESENTATIVENESS AND POSITIVE DISCRIMINATION

LISA LINES

Positive discrimination is the practice or policy of favouring or providing special opportunities for people who are part of a disadvantaged group, in order to attain or promote *equality*. In the US, it is referred to as 'affirmative action'. In the Australian Defence Force (ADF), it is referred to as 'temporary special measures' or 'differential treatment'.

The aim of positive discrimination is to redress an imbalance (or to overcome a disadvantage) that exists in society. The intention of favouring or providing special opportunities for people from disadvantaged groups is not so they will be more advantaged than others, but simply more likely to achieve equality with others. Aristotle wrote: 'There is nothing so unequal as the equal treatment of unequals' – this means that without positive discrimination in certain circumstances, inequality would remain. We can see these ideas at work in many education scholarship programs: financially disadvantaged students are offered free education (and often money for daily expenses) because without this financial assistance they would not have

The Temple of Athena in Athens. Athena was worshipped in ancient Greece as the goddess of war and wisdom.

the same access to education as their wealthier peers.

A major application of positive discrimination in many modern military forces relates to the degree to which women are represented. This positive discrimination aims to help women achieve *equality* with men in the force, and relates to issues of recruitment, retention and career progression of women in the armed forces. Why is this necessary?

In his 1863 Gettysburg Address, Abraham Lincoln famously stated that a democratic government is 'of the people, by the people, for the people'. The military plays a major role in a democratic society by putting into action national policies. So that these actions are being made 'by the people', it is important that the military body represents its society in terms of race, ethnicity, social class, religion and gender. A representative military is also more likely to be recognised as a legitimate arm of the state by society as a whole, which in turn decreases the chances of defence force personnel feeling isolated or alienated from society.

In most modern military forces the constitution of the force does not reflect the makeup of society at large. In Australia, for example, women constitute 51 per cent of the population and 46 per cent of the workforce, but they make up only 14 per cent of personnel in the ADF. Further, the representation of women at senior levels and in certain roles in the ADF is even lower. In 2012, only six of the 182 star-ranked officers in the ADF were women, and of 299 command-level positions, only 26 were occupied by women. Women make up fewer than 3 per cent of ADF aircraft technicians and pilots.

If women in the military were treated exactly the same as men, this situation would not improve. This is because, historically, military forces have been constructed around the male physical standard and tailored to male needs and abilities. Women can and should play an integral role in the military, and it is vital therefore to acknowledge the many ways in which women are disadvantaged or discriminated against (including through sexual harassment) within the traditional military system. Positive discrimination is necessary to improve the elements that make it more difficult for women to enlist, participate equally and be promoted.

One heavily disputed issue that is relevant here is the question of whether women should be allowed to take on combat roles. However, this complex issue is not simply about equality;

there are many other issues involved. Positive discrimination in the military is not about filling a 'quota' of women for political reasons. Rather, it is a practical and strategically important step to maximising a modern military's capabilities and position in society.

Further reading

Dee Gibbon. 2013. 'Beyond Political Correctness: The Capability Argument for Removing Gender Restrictions from Combat Roles in the Australian Defence Force.' *Critical Studies on Security* 1 (2), pp. 253–56.

Lindy Heinecken. 2009. 'A Diverse Society, a Representative Military? The Complexity of Combat Motivation: Designing Personnel Policy to Sustain Capability.' *Australian Army Journal* X (3), pp. 58–78.

Charles Knight. 2013. 'Gender and Sexuality: Sexuality, Cohesion, Masculinity and Managing Diversity in the South African Armed Forces.' *Scientia Militaria, South African Journal of Military Studies* 23, pp. 25–49.

THE MILITARY AND THE MEDIA

DEANE-PETER BAKER

> Journalism and patriotic responsibility are fractious bedfellows
> at the best of times. And war is both the best and worst of
> times for newspapers. Best, because it is real drama and a real
> chance for reporters to achieve fame and fortune. In the huff
> and puff of propaganda and misleading military briefings, the
> journalist can claim the high ground of truth and objectivity.
> And yet it's the worst of times because once one's own soldiers
> are involved, one cannot pretend to have no regard for the
> consequences (Hamilton 2001, 8).

These words by the respected British journalist Adrian Hamilton
sum up, from the perspective of journalists, the ethical challenge
that media engagement with the military poses. Journalists have
a fundamental responsibility to report the truth as objectively as
possible, but at the same time there is a responsibility to ensure
that reporting is responsible, and doesn't cause unnecessary or
undue harm. This challenge is particularly acute when journalists
are engaged in reporting on military operations – the public has
a right to know what is going on, but at the same time careless
reporting can potentially cost lives.

There is more that could be said about the ethical responsibilities of members of the media in engaging with the military, but this book is first and foremost about the ethical responsibilities of military personnel. Military personnel are often suspicious of members of the media, and reluctant to cooperate with them. While the US military's program of embedding journalists with forces in the field in recent decades has improved attitudes somewhat in that force, other nations' armed forces remain hostile. For example, according to the media analyst Kevin Foster, members of the Australian Defence Force remain in general convinced that 'the media's principal reason for wanting access to the battlefield was to sniff out scandal, to smear and to slander' (Foster 2013). While there is undoubtedly some truth to this view, the fact remains that as the armed servants of the state members of the military, and the military itself, are accountable to the citizenry of the state, and the media plays a critical role in assuring that accountability. Put in the terms of Peter Feaver's Agency Theory of civil–military relations (see Chapter 8: Civil-military relations), the media plays the role of a 'fire alarm' which alerts the public and the elected leaders of a democracy to ways in which the military might be 'shirking' its responsibility to serve at the behest of those who the electorate have placed in authority over it. This is an uncomfortable reality for the military, but a reality nonetheless. An honourable military and its personnel will be prepared to bite the bullet and, *genuine* considerations of national security permitting, open themselves to media scrutiny.

That is enough of a challenge in peacetime, but even more difficult in war. The statement, variously attributed to the ancient Greek playwright Aeschylus and the US Senator Hiram Johnson, that 'the first casualty of war is truth', illustrates the depth of the challenge. Deception is a fundamental aspect of military operations. As the great military strategist Carl von Clausewitz wrote,

Memorial marking the place where Lt. Col. 'H' Jones VC, commanding officer of Britain's 2 Para Regiment, was killed in the Battle of Goose Green on 29 May 1982, during the Falklands/Malvinas War. (The photo is taken from the vantage point of the Argentine machine-gun position that fired on and killed Jones – the place he fell is marked with white painted rocks.) On the eve of the battle Jones was horrified to hear the BBC World Service announce that his force was preparing to assault the Argentine positions at Goose Green and Darwin.

'to take the enemy by surprise ... is more or less basic to all operations, for without it superiority at the decisive point is hardly conceivable' (Clausewitz 1984, 198). Deceiving the enemy is, with some exceptions such as perfidy (see Chapter 29: Perfidy and Means *mala in se*) aside, generally an acceptable practice in war, but is it appropriate to mislead the media in order to do so?

The importance of respecting the public's trust in the military is a key, and in most cases, overriding consideration. Where there may be exceptions to the general rule of dealing truthfully with the media, these should be approached with considerable caution, perhaps employing the ethical framework of the doctrine of double effect (see Chapter 25).

References and further reading

Carl von Clausewitz. 1984 [1832]. *On War* (ed. and trans. by Michael Howard and Peter Paret). Princeton University Press.

Peter D. Feaver. 2003. *Armed Servants: Agency, Oversight, and Civil–Military Relations*. Harvard University Press.

Kevin Foster. 2013. 'Looking for Failure? Why the ADF Hates the Australian Media'. *The Conversation* 13 August 2013. Accessed at http://theconversation.com/looking-for-failure-why-the-adf-hates-the-australian-media-16800 [accessed 19 March 2015].

Adrian Hamilton. 2001. 'Media: You Shoot. We Ask the Questions'. *The Independent*, London, 9 October 2001, p. 8.

Tim Markham. 2013. *The Politics of War Reporting: Authority, Authenticity and Morality*. Manchester University Press.

PART THREE
ETHICS WITHIN THE MILITARY PROFESSION

A statue of a US Navy sailor looks on at the battleship USS *Wisconsin* in Norfolk, Virginia, USA.

ROLE MORALITY AND THE UNLIMITED LIABILITY CONTRACT

NIKKI COLEMAN

Society routinely expects different standards of behaviour depending on what role a person has in society. For example, we expect a minister of religion to not be night-clubbing and picking up casual sexual partners, even though it is perfectly legal to do so. We also expect that our elected officials will have a higher standard of behaviour than, say, a used car salesperson, and when our elected officials routinely do not meet these standards it often loses them votes, because their constituents no longer see them as fit for office. Much the same goes for military personnel – society generally expects a higher standard of behaviour from them than is expected of the average citizen.

Stephen Coleman (2013, 38–39) argues that the role morality of the soldier flows from the oath that they take on joining the military; that is, that the soldier promises to serve the state and so is bound by what the state orders them to do. Military values and military virtues will further influence the role morality of the soldier, as will concepts such as Just War Theory, and in particular

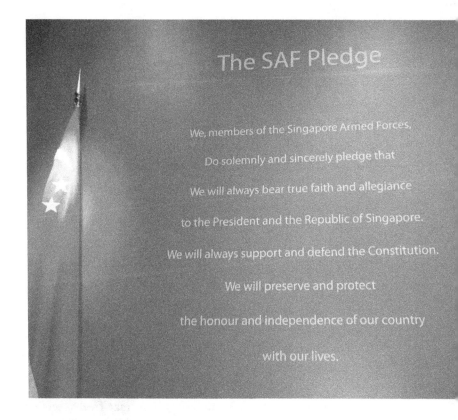

The pledge taken by members of the Singapore Armed Forces on joining the military.

the principles of discrimination and proportionality in *jus in bello* (See Chapters 24 and 26).

If an ordinary citizen were to mete out death and destruction in the same way that a soldier does on the battlefield, he or she would be charged with assault or murder. A soldier does not kill in his or her own name, but rather does so in the name of their state, and so is legally and morally absolved from killing others so long as those deaths occur within the bounds of the principles of *jus in bello* and the Law of Armed Conflict (LOAC). This absolution for what would normally be seen as murder is as a result of the role of the soldier, and is a part of their role morality.

Military members are routinely asked to perform tasks and respond to things that ordinary members of the civilian population are not expected to do. Soldiers are, by definition, asked to kill others, and put themselves at risk of being killed. They are also exposed to significant risk of physical and mental impairment, and have many of their rights taken away from them, simply because they must obey all legal orders. They are routinely unable to refuse medical treatment, and have their normal rights restricted in a range of other ways. In Australia, for example, military personnel are unable to freely speak to the media, join a union, or complain about their working conditions on social media. In the USA they are not able to sue for negligence, and are at times forced to take part in medical experimentation without their consent. One significant argument given in defence of military personnel being required to give up these rights is a utilitarian one; that soldiers sacrifice these rights (and potentially sacrifice their own lives) so that ordinary citizens may freely exercise the same rights.

Another line of argument that is offered as a justification for this situation is a contractual one. According to some theorists, the reason military personnel must obey all legal orders – including those that would under normal circumstances be considered to be in violation of the rights of those following orders – is that they have distinguished themselves from the rest of society by 'signing up' to serve their country, and thus by enlisting have agreed to the what is sometimes called the 'unlimited liability contract' (ULC). This is an implied contract, rather than an explicit legal agreement that military members enter into.

Although the (Australian-born) British General Sir John

Hackett (1910–97) was the first to use the term 'unlimited liability contract', he did not define it, seemingly assuming that his audience fully understood the concept without his expanding on it. The main point that Hackett made about the ULC is that it 'sets the military apart from most other groups' (Hackett 1983, 73). A number of other writers have written briefly on the topic, most notably the distinguished Just War theorist Michael Walzer (1977, 361), who wrote of the loss of freedom and responsibility which comes with enlistment in the military. Walzer asserted that when citizens become soldiers they forfeit certain human rights, particularly the right to life, in exchange for 'soldiers' rights'; that is, that they are immune from prosecution for killing enemy combatants on the battlefield. Warrior-scholar James Dubik (Lieutenant General, US Army (ret.)) counters that the right to life is an inherent 'natural' right that cannot be lost or exchanged, as it is not a right that 'goes with the job' (Dubik 1982, 361–62).

Dubik argues that military personnel retain their 'natural' right to life, and that the government retains its responsibility to ensure that this (and other) rights are protected. Dubik (1982, 363–64) asserts, in contrast to Walzer, that soldiers do not lose or exchange their natural right to life, but rather that soldiers have an increased obligation to protect their fellow citizens, which in turn places soldiers at an increased risk of injury and death. According to Dubik soldiers may be put into morally exceptional circumstances, not because they have relinquished their rights by enlisting, as Walzer maintains, but because they have taken on certain extra moral obligations that ordinary citizens are not bound by. Dubik also argues that officers incur an additional responsibility: 'in addition to being responsible for the control of the means of death and destruction … [they] are directly responsible to the state, and to the soldier to protect the soldier's right to life' (Dubik 1982, 366).

More recently Martin Cook has briefly discussed the idea that there is an implicit commitment between a military officer and their government, such that the members of the military shall serve on terms of unlimited liability and shall 'follow lawful orders in full recognition that they may die or be severely injured in fulfilment of those orders' (Cook 2004, 74). Cook argues that this commitment is 'justified in the mind of the officer because of their moral commitment to the welfare' of their state (Cook 2004, 74). However, Cook's main argument in relation to the concept of unlimited liability, drawing on the work of Hackett, is that it is what separates the military from ordinary citizens, in that it is what makes the military as a profession *sui generis* (that is, unique). This idea that the military is something radically different from a civilian profession, and therefore morally *sui generis* has been challenged by some sociologists such as Morris Janowitz (1960), who argues that the modern military resembles an ordinary occupation, governed by market principles, and is no longer seen as a life of service. If military service has become something akin to an ordinary career, it seems difficult to sustain the argument that it is morally *sui generis* – that the moral norms and principles that apply to ordinary civilians cannot be coherently applied to the military. However, this view of the unlimited liability commitment as being 'the distinctive feature of the military profession *vis-à-vis* other professions' (Orme 2011, 24) remains influential.

References and further reading

Stephen Coleman. 2013. *Military Ethics: An Introduction with Case Studies.* Oxford University Press.

Martin L. Cook. 2004. *The Moral Warrior: Ethics and Service in the U.S. Military.* State University of New York Press.

James Dubik. 1982. 'Human Rights, Command Responsibility,

and Walzer's Just War Theory'. *Philosophy & Public Affairs*, 11 (4), pp. 354–71.

John Winthrop Hackett. 1983. *The Profession of Arms*. Macmillan.

Morris Janowitz. 1960. *The Professional Soldier: A Social and Political Portrait*. Macmillan.

C.W. Orme. 2011. *Beyond Compliance: Professionalism, Trust and Capability in the Australian Profession of Arms (Report of the ADF Personal Conduct Review)*. Commonwealth of Australia.

Michael Walzer. 1977. *Just and Unjust Wars: A Moral Argument with Historical Illustrations*. Basic Books.

THE TRIANGULAR BALANCE

DEANE-PETER BAKER

There are few responsibilities as weighty as those that rest on the shoulders of today's military leaders. For one thing, the forces they command have a capacity for destruction that is arguably unprecedented in history. The potential killing power inherent in the highly efficient weapons systems that today's military forces can bring to bear brings with it the responsibility of ensuring that those weapons are used in a way that risks as little harm as possible to non-combatants and non-military infrastructure. At the same time, for all the advances that have been made in stand-off weaponry and precision targeting, we have yet to reach the point (and may never reach it) where it is no longer necessary to put 'boots on the ground' in order to achieve mission success. So there is another responsibility here that military leaders must balance against the first one: the responsibility to protect the lives of the soldiers, sailors, airmen and marines that they lead. And both of these responsibilities must again be balanced against the responsibility to complete the mission at hand. As former US Navy SEAL Dick Couch puts it:

There are three considerations that are never far from the

Memorial to Major General Sir Edward Woodgate (1845–1900),
British Army, who was killed in the Battle of Spion Kop during the
second Anglo-Boer War. It is rare that senior officers are killed in
the front line of battle – the greater challenge is balancing the
responsibilities of achieving the mission, protecting the lives of
subordinates and minimising the risk of harm to non-combatants.

mind of a commander in an active theater who has squads and
platoons in the field:

The value of the target – collectively, the mission

The risk to his own troops

The risk to noncombatant civilians

A lot of time and attention, and no small amount of lost sleep,

go into balancing these issues, both the tactical considerations
as well as moral considerations (Couch 2010, xvii).

These three competing responsibilities of mission, own troops
and non-combatants are sometimes referred to collectively as *the
triangular balance*. (This should not be confused with the method
of Ethical Triangulation outlined in Chapter 6.) The great challenge lies in the fact that in practice these responsibilities are
interconnected, and pull against one another. If, say, a commander
puts a premium on protecting his own troops, then either the
mission will suffer – as has allegedly happened in some UN
peacekeeping operations in which troop contingent commanders have effectively kept their troops in relatively safe base areas
rather than going out on patrol (see, for example, Howden 2011)
– or else non-combatants will suffer as risky patrols are replaced
by the use of 'reconnaissance by fire' and similar methods. If, on
the other hand, a commander puts achieving the mission above
all else, this could have the effect of putting his or her troops and
non-combatants at great risk. Finally, if the decision is made to
bring the risk of harm to non-combatants to as close to zero as
possible, this may either mean that the mission cannot be carried
out at all, or only at the expense of imposing very significant risks
onto those who must execute the mission orders.

Ultimately, then, it is up to the commander on the spot to
work out the appropriate balance between these three competing priorities. There is no hard and fast rule to apply here, and it
is, in the end a matter of wisdom. That said, an important factor
that must be taken into consideration is the nature of the overall
mission. If, for example, the mission is a humanitarian intervention aimed at preventing the mass killing of non-combatants, it is
clearly counter-productive and inappropriate for the intervening
force to shift the majority of the risk entailed in the intervention

onto the civilian population that they have ostensibly come to rescue. In a war for national survival, on the other hand, it might well be acceptable (albeit painfully regrettable) to push more of the risk onto non-combatants in order to ensure that the mission can be accomplished.

What the above examples illustrate is that there are circumstances that bring two of these three competing priorities into closer alignment than would otherwise be the case. In a desperate war of national survival where the results of mission failure could be catastrophic, protecting the force becomes an essential feature of mission success. By contrast, in a counter-insurgency war, where the support of the local population is vital to mission success it is the counter-insurgency forces that must accept the greater risk.

Broadly speaking one way of understanding the triangular balance is that it is a summary of what the proportionality requirement of the *jus in bello* (see Chapter 26) looks like from the perspective of the individual commander. It is without question one of the most challenging ethical aspects of the employment of military force, and a key reason why military personnel cannot simply be capable 'technicians of violence' but must also be deeply ethically aware.

References and further reading

Dick Couch. 2010. *A Tactical Ethic*. Naval Institute Press.

Daniel Howden. 2011. 'UN Accused of Standing by While Sudanese Forces Kill Civilians'. *The Independent* Friday 8 July 2011. Accessed at www.independent.co.uk/news/world/africa/un-accused-of-standing-by-while-sudanese-forces-killed-civilians-2308896.html [accessed 18 March 2015].

14 FAIRNESS AND JUSTICE

PETER BALINT

Most of us get pretty upset when we believe we've been treated unfairly. That's true in ordinary life, but perhaps even more so in military life where so much more of an individual's existence is tied into his or her profession and unfairness potentially bites a lot deeper. Calling something unfair or unjust is a harsh moral judgment. Of course, as the cliché goes 'life isn't fair', but this does not mean it shouldn't be, nor that we shouldn't strive to make it as fair as it can be.

Fairness or justice (in this chapter I will treat them as the same thing) can be understood in several different ways. Often issues of unfairness arise when rules are either not applied, or are applied inconsistently. So, for example, if a colleague has equivalent experience and qualifications to you yet gets a promotion ahead of you, or if another colleague is granted additional leave when the only relevant difference between you and them is that they are friends with the commanding officer, then we appear to have clear-cut cases of unfairness.

What is wrong in these examples is that like cases have not

been treated alike. This is a basic and important understanding of justice, and one which dates right back to the Ancient Greek philosopher Aristotle (384–322 BC). In these cases the question is not whether the rules themselves are fair, but whether they have been applied fairly; that is, by only taking relevant factors into consideration. This is where the phrase 'justice is blind' comes from – to be just is to only see what is directly relevant and be blind to all other factors.

While this captures much of we mean by justice or fairness, there is also the important question of whether a particular set of rules, or a practice or an institution is itself just. How, for example, should leave be arranged in a military environment? How should duties and privileges be distributed among a particular group of personnel? If a particular resource is scarce, who should get it?

A common answer both inside and outside the military is that it is all up to merit or talent. That is, when determining 'who gets what' – the question of *distributive justice* – only merit should count. This idea of *meritocracy* has much going for it, especially in a military environment where it is not only an issue of justice, but also of capability.

But the question of merit is not so straightforward (and is quite different from the issue of *desert*, that is, the issue of getting what we deserve). There are two types of problem with saying a fair system is simply one that rewards merit. First, while it is true that we want the best people for particular roles, there is a question of whether people have had a *fair opportunity* to develop their talents. A military might, for example, need to choose one person out of two candidates for a prestigious role as a marksperson for international shooting competitions. Given that the role involves specialist shooting abilities, they should choose the best shot. But when should this choice be made? It could, for example, be made upon recruitment, in which case the person who grew up on a farm with plenty of opportunity to practise shooting would likely be chosen ahead of the person who grew up in the city and who had hardly ever touched firearms. In this case, we might say only one person has had a fair opportunity to develop their talents – and some might even argue that the person who grew up in the city has been treated unfairly.

An alternative is to offer both candidates the same training and to choose the best candidate after they have both been adequately trained. In this case both candidates will have had a fair opportunity to develop their talents. Indeed this is what usually happens. In many branches of modern militaries, specialisation occurs only after foundation training. Not only does this help with capability, but it also treats military personnel fairly by cancelling out as much as possible any background circumstances that may give one candidate an unfair advantage over another.

The second problem with merit is that not all issues of distributive justice involve merit. While merit – with or without adjusting for background circumstances – is relevant for roles and rewards, it has no relevance for what we think of as *rights* or basic protections. Take, for example, the idea that if you are injured at work you should be compensated. This is a right that is not dependent on how talented you are.

The idea of *egalitarianism* might help here. At its most basic, egalitarianism is the idea that we are we all morally equal and should all enjoy equal rights. Many egalitarians go further and say the enjoyment of these rights requires that we are all treated roughly the same in some more substantive manner. So while the first type of egalitarian will see people having their basic rights violated as unjust, this other type of egalitarians will see, for example, too much economic inequality as also unjust.

There are many varieties of this more substantive type of egalitarianism; with some arguing for equal *resources*, some for equal

A municipal building in Dijon, France. A commitment to egalitarianism is captured in France's national slogan of '*liberté, égalité, fraternité*'.

opportunities, some for equal *welfare*, and some for a distribution of resources that favours the worst off (*the difference principle*). While these concerns are more to do with *social justice*, egalitarianism is relevant to the military and can be used to guide policy on questions like pay and conditions.

So far I've outlined a few principles to help decide 'who gets what', but let me end with the most famous method of determining this question. One of the problems with determining the right answer is that we are all self-interested and all have particular views about the world, and so our answer will reflect – either consciously or unconsciously – these sources of bias.

The 20th-century American political philosopher John Rawls (1921–2002) tries to remove these sources of bias, and asks us to imagine designing the rules for our society if we somehow didn't know what our talents, skin colour, gender, interests, religion, etc. were going to be (Rawls 1971). Under this *veil of ignorance*, he imagines that not only would we avoid designing a society that favoured us, we would be careful to design a society in which the worst off were as well off as possible – this is because we might just end up being that person with the severe disadvantages. Rawls's *original position* latches onto the idea of justice being blind – a fair set of rules are ones where nobody has had the opportunity to advantage themselves in their creation.

Rawls argues that two principles would emerge from this hypothetical situation. First, there is what he calls the *liberty principle*. Here the idea is that when it comes to essential freedoms and rights we think of as essential to all human beings we should be egalitarian – that is, everyone should have the same equal access to those freedoms and rights. Rawls's second principle deals with the question of the fair arrangement of social and economic differences between people. It's a two-part principle. The first part is composed of a principle that I mentioned earlier, *the difference principle*. Here the idea is that inequalities are allowed (for example, inequalities in pay), to allow for people to 'get ahead' on the basis of *merit*, so long as the difference that arises also has an effect of making things better for the worst off. The clearest example of the application of this principle in society is through the mechanism of taxation – those who are successful in their careers are allowed to benefit from their endeavours, but in so doing they must pay tax, which is used to help those who are (economically and socially) in the bottom layer of society. The second part of the principle offers an important proviso to add to the difference principle, and is called the principle of *fair equality of opportunity*. Simply put, the idea here is that the social and economic inequalities that the difference principle allows for are only acceptable when everyone has had a fair opportunity to 'get ahead' in the first place (as I discussed earlier).

References and further reading

Ronald Dworkin. 1978. *Taking Rights Seriously*. Harvard University Press.

Ronald Dworkin. 2013. *Justice for Hedgehogs*. Belknap Press.

John Rawls. 1971. *A Theory of Justice*. Belknap Press.

Michael J. Sandel. 2007. *Justice: A Reader*. Oxford University Press.

Michael J. Sandel. 2010. *Justice: What's the Right Thing to Do?* Farrar, Straus and Giroux.

RIGHTS

DEANE-PETER BAKER

The idea that humans have rights has become widely accepted in the period since the Second World War, a war characterised by so many horrifying human rights violations that it led to the drafting and adoption of the Universal Declaration of Human Rights by the United Nations in 1948. For all this general agreement, however, the concept of rights, and the question of which rights actually exist, remains highly contested. And there are some, including distinguished and respected scholars and thinkers, who reject at least some formulations of the idea of rights, agreeing with Jeremy Bentham (see Chapter 2: Consequentialist ethics), who famously declared the notion to be 'nonsense upon stilts'.

An important distinction to make is that between legal rights and natural rights. Legal rights are acquired as a consequence of particular and context-specific political, social and legal arrangements. In Australia, for example, citizens have a right to publically funded health care, but Australians don't have that same right in most of the other countries of the world that they might travel to, and it is a right that could, in principle, cease to exist in Australia were there a significant change to existing government policy. This kind of right is relatively uncontroversial. The

View of the Eiffel Tower from the Palais de Chaillot in Paris, where the Universal Declaration of Human Rights was signed into effect in 1948.

idea of natural or human rights, on the other hand, is far more contested (it is this conception of rights that Bentham objected to so strongly).

What makes natural rights different from legal rights is that they are deemed not to be contingent (dependent) on any particular social, political or legal arrangements, but are instead considered to be inherent in human beings. (There is a significant debate over whether other living creatures and even some inanimate objects might be considered to have natural rights, but we don't have space to consider that debate here.) Consider, for example, the widely held belief that humans have a right to life. This is held to be an intrinsic feature of being human, not something that is dependent on some or other government or other body granting that right. Probably the most influential proponent of natural rights was the Christian theologian and philosopher Thomas Aquinas (1225–74). Many religious thinkers have followed Aquinas in viewing natural rights as being a consequence of humanity having been created by God; however, there are also many non-religious supporters of natural rights who see them arising out of human nature, or being simply a matter of logic.

Rights and duties often go hand in hand. For example, an individual's right to life imposes on everyone else a duty not to kill that person (this is sometimes called a 'claim right', because it is a right that entails there being a claim on others). Sometimes, however, rights have no corresponding duties. My right to free speech imposes no claim on anyone else – you have no duty, for example, to listen to me. (Such a right is referred to as a 'liberty right', or sometimes, a 'privilege'.) Of course, my right to freedom from assault does come into play here, and imposes a claim on you, as you have a duty not to physically force me to shut up no matter how much you dislike what I have to say!

Even if natural or human rights do exist (and again, there is widespread agreement that they do, despite disagreements over the extent of these rights and their metaphysical basis), that does not mean that they are necessarily absolute. My right to freedom of speech can be limited if doing so is necessary to avoid a sufficiently serious harm. The classic example that is usually used to illustrate this is that my right to freedom of speech does not extend as far as allowing me to shout 'Fire!' in a crowded theatre when there is no fire, for this might cause a panic which could cause some of the theatre-goers to be hurt.

The military profession is one, perhaps more than any other, which gives rise to circumstances that are held to justify significant curtailments on the rights of those who are members of the profession. The most obvious cases relate to the right to life. Under normal circumstances a person cannot be killed without violating her right to life, except in a very limited set of circumstances in which she is held to have *forfeited* (or given up) her right to life. Imagine, for example, that Jenny decides, in a jealous rage, to stab Martin to death. In the moment that Jenny is thrusting her blade towards Martin he does not violate Jenny's right to life if he draws his gun and shoots her dead. We say of such circumstances that Martin has acted in self-defence, and that he did not violate Jenny's right to life because, in choosing to try to kill Martin, she had forfeited her right to life. Martin, of course, may only attempt to kill Jenny if doing so is absolutely necessary to save his own life, and only for as long as the threat exists. During times of war, however, things look rather different for military personnel and other combatants. It is generally held that in war military personnel may, without committing a human rights violation, kill enemy combatants wherever they are found and regardless of what they are doing. (There are some restrictions that apply to this general statement, which are discussed in Chapters 24: The principle of discrimination/distinction, and 27: Surrender and detention.) It seems therefore that the right of military personnel not to be killed is significantly curtailed during times of war, well beyond what would normally be justified by the mere exercise of the right to self-defence (for an in-depth analysis of the relationship between war and self-defence, as well as a comprehensive discussion of rights and duties, see Rodin 2005).

It is not only during times of war that members of the military profession find their rights curtailed, this is also a feature of peacetime service. In several countries, for example (often countries with a history of military coups), the importance of maintaining appropriate civil–military relations (see Chapter 8) is held to justify restricting some or all members of the military from any political involvement – even voting in elections – for the duration of their military service. A more common example is the impact of military service on freedom of speech. Issues of national security are such that, even in peacetime, military personnel are far more restricted in what they may say about aspects of their work than civilians generally are. Few would doubt that some restrictions on rights are justified, even in peacetime, for military personnel. But because rights matter, these restrictions must be genuinely necessary, otherwise they are simply forms of abuse.

Regardless of what one thinks of the metaphysical underpinnings of the idea of human rights, it would be hard to argue that the concept is without merit, and there can be no doubt that the notion of human rights has become a vitally important conceptual tool in the fight against gratuitous and unjustifiable harms being inflicted on defenceless people in myriad circumstances around the globe. As a consequence, military personnel operate under a weighty moral duty to do all they can to respect the basic human rights of non-combatants and captured enemy personnel, and leaders of military forces have an equally weighty duty to ensure that the rights of those who serve are not overridden or curtailed without genuine justification.

References and further reading

Simon Blackburn (2009). *Ethics: A Very Short Introduction.* Oxford University Press.

David Rodin. 2005. *War and Self-Defense.* Oxford University Press.

Philip Schofield. 2003. 'Jeremy Bentham's "Nonsense upon Stilts"'. *Utilitas* 15 (1), pp. 1–26.

ILLEGAL ORDERS AND WHISTLE-BLOWING

DEANE-PETER BAKER

Late 1945 saw the start of an International Military Tribunal, which took place in Nuremberg, Germany. It was the most famous of the so-called Nuremberg Trials, which held senior members of the Nazi regime accountable for their actions during and prior to the Second World War. This military tribunal famously ended any doubt on a very important issue related to the conduct of military personnel – never again can any well-informed soldier, sailor, airman or marine seriously claim that they are innocent of wrongdoing because they were 'just following orders'.

It is certainly true that military personnel have a legal responsibility to follow orders from those in authority over them; however this responsibility is only attached to legal orders. The reverse is true when it comes to illegal orders – military personnel have a firm moral responsibility to *not* carry out illegal orders. Of course most military personnel are not lawyers or experts in the law, so on some occasions it may be difficult to ascertain whether an order is legal or not. Where circumstances allow, such legally ambiguous orders should be resisted until legal clarity is attained. In many cases, however, illegal orders are clearly so. As a general rule of thumb, if an order breaks a fundamental principle of morality, such as the prohibition against inflicting harm on the innocent, there's a good chance that it is also illegal.

What, practically speaking, should someone in the military do if they are given an illegal order? What is appropriate is a matter of wisdom and is largely dictated by the circumstances. In some cases it might be possible to simply ignore the order. However, while this allows the person receiving the order to keep his or her hands clean, it leaves open the possibility that the person or persons giving the illegal orders will order other subordinates to do illegal acts which might then be carried out. In most cases, therefore, it will be necessary to not only refuse to carry out the

The Nuremberg Palace of Justice, where the Nuremberg Trials were held between 1945 and 1949.

order in question, but also to take positive steps to ensure that the person or persons giving the illegal orders are held accountable. In most cases this will involve reporting the illegal order through the appropriate military channels. In some rare cases, however, where that is not possible or proves ineffective, it might be necessary to resort to circumventing the military chain of command and going directly to someone like a responsible government official or even to the media. For example, the massacre that was carried out by US troops (many of whom claimed they were 'just following orders') at My Lai in Vietnam in 1968 was reported up the chain of command by Warrant Officer Hugh Thompson (a helicopter pilot who both observed the massacre and, with his crew, intervened to stop some of the killing), but the report was ignored by Thompson's superiors. The massacre was only finally investigated after another soldier, Specialist Ronald L. Ridenhour wrote a letter to 30 members of the US Congress. Even then the massacre might not have come to light – all but three of the Congressmen that Ridenhour wrote to ignored his letter.

Ridenhour is an example of what is commonly referred to as a 'whistle-blower'. In a widely quoted definition Janet Near and Marcia Miceli explain that whistle-blowing is 'the disclosure by organization members (former or current) of illegal, immoral, or illegitimate practices under the control of their employers, to persons or organizations that may be able to effect action' (Near and Miceli 1985, 4). While whistle-blowing has become more socially accepted in recent years, there are many who still consider the practice to be morally reprehensible. People who hold this view often consider whistle-blowers to be disloyal, destructive and self-promoting. What should we make of this view? It is certainly true that whistle-blowers can cause significant damage by their actions. For example, Edward Snowden, the former NSA contractor who leaked tens or hundreds of thousands of classified

A Vietnam War-era 'Huey' helicopter, like the one flown by Warrant Officer Hugh Thompson.

documents to the media, undoubtedly damaged US interests, undermined aspects of US national security, and may also have put lives at risk. This risk of damage means that potential whistle-blowers should weigh up whether or not the potential damage caused by their revelations outweighs the good gained from them, and should furthermore be certain that public disclosure is the last reasonable resort available to them. The question of motive is important here. If one is motivated to blow the whistle under some self-serving rationale, such as a desire for public attention or a desire to gain revenge, there is a far greater chance that the requirements of proportionality and last resort will not be met.

What of the claim that whistle-blowers are disloyal? Snowden, for example, has been called a traitor, which is at heart a claim that he has betrayed an important trust, that he has been disloyal. Whether or not that is an appropriate characterisation of Snowden's actions, it is certainly true that some who blow the whistle are disloyal, particularly if in so doing they are acting on inappropriate motives and fail to consider proportionality and last resort. However, when whistle-blowers are motivated by a desire to see justice done and carry out their actions appropriately, the charge of disloyalty is misplaced. In the military context loyalty is usually a fiercely defended value, which has led to some advocating the principle 'loyalty above all else, except justice'. The problem with this principle is that it seems to accept that the whistle-blower who is acting in the cause of justice must at the same time accept that he or she is being disloyal. But this is mistaken because it mistakes the appropriate locus of loyalty. As Wim Vandekerckhove and M.S. Ronald Commers write, 'the object of loyalty is not the physicality of an organization', or, we might add, the people who make up that organisation, 'but its corpus of explicit mission statement, goals, value statement and code of conduct' (Vandekerckhove and Commers 2004, 225). In the case of the military, the appropriate object of loyalty is to those principles and values that justify the military's existence and actions, as discussed elsewhere in this book. If a whistle-blower acts appropriately to expose a corruption of those principles within a military organisation, then he or she is behaving in a way that is more loyal than those who are responsible for that corruption. Whistle-blowers are often isolated and shunned, and their actions can often come at a very significant personal cost. Except where it is the product of inappropriate motivation, or where it is carried out rashly, whistle-blowing is an honourable act that requires considerable moral courage on the part of the whistle-blower.

References and further reading

George G. Brenkert. 2012. 'Whistle-Blowing, Moral Integrity, and Organizational Ethics', in *The Oxford Handbook of Business Ethics* (George G. Brenkert, ed.). Oxford University Press, pp. 563–601.

Janet Near and Marcia Miceli. 1985. 'Organizational Dissidence: The Case of Whistle-Blowing'. *Journal of Business Ethics* 4, pp. 1–16.

Wim Vandekerckhove and M.S. Ronald Commers, 'Whistle Blowing and Rational Loyalty'. 2004. *Journal of Business Ethics* 53 (1/2), pp. 225–33.

PART FOUR
GOING TO WAR AND ENDING WARS

The aircraft carrier USS *Yorktown* at Patriot's Point, South Carolina, USA.

PACIFISM

NED DOBOS

Pacifism in its most recognisable form is an absolute, principled condemnation of violence. From Jesus' entreaty to 'turn the other cheek', Christian pacifists infer that inflicting physical harm on others – even in self-defence – is contrary to the teachings of their faith and therefore forbidden. Mohandas Gandhi (1869–1948) treated *ahimsa* or non-violence as part of a larger project of spiritual self-transformation. In a similar vein, Dr Martin Luther King Jr (1929–68) saw merit in being victimised without retaliating: 'unearned suffering is redemptive', he was once quoted saying. A more moderate form of pacifism objects not to violence *per se*, but specifically to the organised, politically driven, large-scale killing and maiming that characterises warfare. Hence, Jenny Teichman (1986) refers to this variety of pacifism as 'anti-war-ism'.

The distinctive feature of these 'absolute' forms of pacifism is that they reject the idea – taken for granted by Just War theorists – that waging war is sometimes morally acceptable as the lesser of two evils. The absolute pacifist denies that Just War Theory accurately captures the demands of morality insofar as it licenses mass killing under *any* conceivable circumstances.

Not surprisingly, this position has failed to gain much traction with philosophers of war and military ethicists, for whom Just War Theory remains the most intuitively plausible and theoretically coherent framework for evaluating armed conflict. In recent years, however, a new kind of pacifism has begun to emerge: one which, rather than contesting Just War Theory, embraces it. According to so-called 'contingent' pacifism, war is indeed morally acceptable if it satisfies the requirements of Just War Theory (just cause; proportionality; last resort, etc.). However, no actual war meets these requirements; they are simply not achievable given certain empirical realities. Therefore, while war can *in theory* be justified, *as a matter of fact* it never is. On this view, Just War Theory – when properly interpreted and applied – leads to a pacifist conclusion.

A man sits on a bench in front of a mosaic calling for peace, in the war-divided town of Nicosia, Cyprus.

There are a number of different paths to contingent pacifism. Indeed, for each of the familiar principles of Just War Theory, there is a powerful argument that, given the kinds of wars that are fought nowadays and the kinds of people that fight them, those principles are never satisfied in the 'real world'.

Some scholars think that the kinds of wars fought nowadays simply do not satisfy the 'just cause' requirement. David Rodin (2002), for instance, argues that while it may be permissible to wage war in order to repel an invader that is intent on exterminating us, most wars of national self-defence are not waged to resist this kind of genocidal aggression. Rather, they are waged to protect our political interests, such as our sovereignty and

A Vietnam War-era 105mm howitzer. Early opposition to the Vietnam War in the United States grew into a powerful anti-war movement. Many who were opposed to the war espoused pacifism, while others objected to the Vietnam War in particular, often for reasons reflected in the principles of Just War Theory.

territorial integrity, as well as our economic welfare. Are these interests important enough to justify killing the people who threaten them? Rodin insists that they are not. Hence, wars of national self-defence are typically not justified: an attack on our political and economic interests is not a 'just cause'.

Other contingent pacifists maintain that modern war is never justified because it never satisfies the Just War principle of 'right intention'. According to this principle, if a war is being driven by ulterior motives – such as economic and political advantage, revenge, ethnic hatred, and so on – that war is unjustified even if a just cause happens to be objectively present (for in this case the just cause functions as a mere pretence). A number of recent publications suggest, in effect, that right intention is always absent these days, given the prevailing structures of political power and the kinds of people that invariably win office. Andrew Fiala's *The Just War Myth* (2007) and David Keen's *Useful Enemies: When Waging Wars is More Important than Winning Them* (2012) are two noteworthy examples here. The former emphasises the political incentives for war, while the latter suggests that war is and always has been a racket waged for its profitability above all else.

Perhaps the most common form of contingent pacifism rests on the observation that, given that wars are increasingly being fought in built-up urban areas with mechanised weapons and aerial bombardment, it is inevitable that some innocent civilians will be harmed. Classical Just War Theory does make allowances for civilian casualties as long they are merely a foreseen side effect of an attack on a legitimate military target, rather than intended as a means or as an end. Here we have the so-called 'doctrine of double effect' (see Chapter 25). This doctrine has been subject to much critical pressure, however. The distinction between intention and foresight upon which it relies has been dismissed by many thinkers as morally irrelevant. If I speed down the road knowing for certain, but not intending, that I will strike and kill a pedestrian at the crossing, is this really any different, morally speaking, from deliberately running down the pedestrian? If the doctrine of double effect is implausible, then killing civilians with 'mere foresight' is no better than intentionally killing them. And if intentionally killing civilians is absolutely forbidden, then so too is killing them incidentally (as 'collateral damage'). And if all modern war can be expected to produce collateral damage, then all modern war is forbidden. Once again, pacifism is the conclusion.

Both absolute pacifism and contingent pacifism object to the waging of war. A third kind of pacifism – so-called *institutional* pacifism – has a different focus. The institutional pacifist objects not so much to waging wars with the military resources that we have amassed; he objects to the amassing of those resources to begin with. To put it another way, while absolute and contingent pacifists object to military *operations*, institutional pacifists object to the very existence of the military. Interestingly, some proponents of this view are willing to accept that individual acts of war might be permissible; they simply deny that this is sufficient to justify the state in creating and maintaining a war-making machine, especially since there are (they believe) alternative arrangements for national defence that are equally effective and less costly in both human and material terms. There is an important insight here: the moral status of any given war, and the moral status of the structures that make it possible, though related, are independent matters.

References and further reading

Deane-Peter Baker. 2015. 'Epistemic Uncertainty and Excusable Wars'. *The Philosophical Forum* 46 (1), pp. 55–70.

Ned Dobos. 2016. *The New Pacifism: Just War in the Real World*. Oxford University Press.

Andrew Fiala. 2007. *The Just War Myth: The Moral Illusions of War*. Rowman & Littlefield.

David Keen. 2012. *Useful Enemies: When Waging Wars is More Important than Winning Them*. Yale University Press.

David Rodin. 2002. *War and Self-Defense*. Oxford University Press.

Jenny Teichman. 1986. *Pacifism and the Just War*. Blackwell.

REALISM

NED DOBOS

There are two varieties of political realism: descriptive (or factual), and prescriptive (or normative). According to descriptive realism, states are, *as a matter of fact,* motivated exclusively by national self-interest. Their behaviour is not influenced by moral considerations. On this view, any appeal to ideology and values in world politics is mere rhetoric, concealing the pursuit of power, which is at the root of every decision taken in the international arena. Some see this as an inevitable consequence of human nature. Since humans are naturally self-seeking, the argument goes, it is to be expected that this will be reflected in their political institutions. For 'structural' realists, by contrast, it is the anarchical nature of the international system – the absence of an 'overarching sovereign' or 'world government' – that explains why states are so preoccupied with their own interests. The absence of a world government makes for an insecure environment which forces states to seek power in order to ensure their own survival.

Prescriptive (or normative) realism, on the other hand, says that even if states *do* behave morally sometimes, they *shouldn't.* States *ought* to make decisions based exclusively on the national interest. Moral considerations – of right and wrong, justice and injustice, fairness and unfairness, decency and indecency – have no place in political decision-making at the international level. Interestingly, prescriptive realists often defend their position on distinctly moral grounds. Some suggest that an 'ethical' foreign policy is fraught with danger and is likely to produce pernicious consequences. They say that the surest route to universal peace and happiness is in fact universal national egoism, where all states concentrate exclusively on their own wealth and power. At work here is an 'indirect utilitarian' logic: consciously striving for good outcomes produces bad outcomes. Good outcomes are more effectively promoted when everybody acts selfishly. George F. Kennan (1904–2005), for instance, wrote:

> It is a curious thing ... that the legalistic approach to world affairs, rooted as it unquestionably is in a desire to do away with war and violence, makes violence more enduring, more terrible, and more destructive to political stability than did the older motives of the national interest. A war fought in the name of high moral principle finds no early end short of some form of total domination. (Kennan 1951, 101)

Kennan believes that the best way to maximise global well-being is for states to maximise their own interests, and he is not alone in this respect. The high-priest of post-war realism, Hans J. Morgenthau (1904–1980), blamed 'sentimentalism' in foreign policy for the fact that 'political success has been sacrificed without appreciable gain in universal morality'. According to Morgenthau, states lack both the will and the resources to pursue moral objectives to completion. As a result, 'moralistic' doctrines are only ever implemented in 'fits and starts ... here half-heartedly and with insufficient means, there with all-out military commitments, there not at all...' (Morgenthau 1951, 114). This leads to a suboptimal outcome in terms of the national interest, without

Battlefield debris from the Falklands/Malvinas War on Mt Harriett, East Falkland. Realists adopt a position on war that echoes General William Tecumseh Sherman's famous statement during the American Civil War that 'war is cruelty, and you cannot refine it'.

producing global benefits substantial enough to offset this sacrifice. The result is negative net utility overall.

This argument for prescriptive realism is consequentialist or utilitarian in nature. It is concerned with prescribing norms that will deliver the 'greatest happiness of the greatest number'. An alternative argument for prescriptive realism is deontological in character. Crudely, it says that a government breaches the trust of its own constituents by making foreign policy decisions based on anything but the national interest. In the international arena, where there is no overarching sovereign capable of enforcing rules of peaceful cooperation, it is reasonable (so this argument goes) to expect that each community will seek power in order to bolster its own security. In this highly competitive setting, a nation that allows moral considerations to interfere with its pursuit of power puts itself in danger by allowing potential aggressors to acquire a relative advantage in terms of position and resources, which can then be translated into a military advantage. This is a risk, prescriptive realists contend, that no political community can be obliged to take. We cannot be duty-bound to put our collective survival in jeopardy. Therefore, according to prescriptive realists, each nation is at liberty to promote its interests unfettered by moral constraints, and to empower an agent (the government) to do this on its behalf. This gives the government a fiduciary obligation to advance the national interest by any means necessary. Those are the terms of the social contract between the people and their government. Morgenthau puts it this way:

> The individual may say for himself: '*Fiat justitia, pereat mundus* (Let justice be done, even if the worlds perish),' but the state has no right to say so in the name of those who are in its care. Both individual and state must judge political action by universal moral principles, such as that of liberty. Yet while the individual has a moral right to sacrifice himself in defence of such a moral principle, the state has no right to let its moral disapprobation of the infringement of liberty get in the way of successful political action, itself inspired by the moral principle of national survival. (Morgenthau and Thompson 1985, 166)

What Morgenthau is saying is that the primary responsibility of any government is to ensure the security and well-being of its citizens, and morality's intrusion into foreign policy interferes with the fulfilment of this responsibility. He thus reaches the conclusion that states have an obligation to act purely in the national interest, without regard to moral considerations.

References and further reading

George Kennan. 1951. *American Diplomacy 1900–1950.* University of Chicago Press.

Hans J. Morgenthau. 1951. *In Defense of the National Interest: A Critical Examination of American Foreign Policy.* Knopf.

Hans Morgenthau and Kenneth Thompson. 1985. *Politics Among Nations.* Sixth edition. McGraw-Hill.

JUS AD BELLUM (JUST WAR THEORY)

ANTHONY BURKE

The *jus ad bellum* (literally 'right to war') is the set of rules governing the resort to force: when war may be waged, for what purposes, and under what conditions. It imposes a test of legitimacy – moral, political or legal – which must be met. It is distinguished from the *jus in bello* (see Part Five) in that it is primarily concerned with the resort to war rather than its conduct, although it also prescribes general principles about that. The Just War Tradition links the *jus ad bellum* and the *jus in bello* together as important guides and tests for force, insisting that both sets of rules be met for a conflict to be legitimate. Recent scholarship within the tradition has also added the categories of *jus ex bello* and *jus post bellum* which add further requirements for a war to be considered to be just (see Chapter 23).

International law, which has been strongly informed by the Just War Tradition, is more ambiguous. On the one hand, the International Humanitarian Law (IHL) contained in the Geneva Conventions and Protocols and a number of other weapons treaties, sets out rules for the conduct of war in great detail but is morally agnostic about the resort to force: this is simply a right that accrues to actors through the 'combatant's privilege'. On the other, the United Nations Charter sets out conditions for the legitimate and lawful resort to force between states – violations of which may soon be a major international crime if amendments to the Rome Statute of the International Criminal Court that define the crime of 'aggression' come into effect after 2017. However, nothing in international law prevents a government using force within its own borders, or a non-state group beginning a campaign of violence or terror. The role of international law in force short of war – such as deterrence, coercive diplomacy or sanctions – is unclear, but legal opinion is of the view that cyber-attacks, especially when they result in actual damage to property and human beings, are a form of force and are regulated by law (Gray 2004, 60–94; Burke et. al. 2014, 88–93; Schmitt et. al. 2013, 3).

Just War Theory states seven key criteria for the resort to force. The first two state that war must be waged with the 'right intention' and in a 'just cause'. Rather than being waged for revenge or power-seeking, war should only be waged in self-defence, defence of others, for the restoration of rights, or to prevent and punish a wrong. It should also be a 'last resort', and have 'a proportionality of ends', so that the overall harm caused is less than the wrong being righted. This is an application of Thomas Aquinas's notion of the 'double effect', and critics have argued it lends itself to overly expansive interpretations that could support military adventurism. The war should also have 'a reasonable chance of success' – one should not risk civilian and military life, along with costs to the treasury, without it – and be decided upon by a 'right authority'. It should also be 'publicly declared' (Bellamy 2006, Ch. 6). Formal declarations of war are rarely made now, and immense controversy exists over who a 'right authority' is. Is it a state – and within that, is it a prime minister or president, a cabinet, or

The Kuwait Towers, seen through a wrecked building in Kuwait City. The United Nations authorised war to drive the invading Iraqi forces out of Kuwait in 1991. This war, the Gulf War, is seen by many analysts as a rare example of a modern war that meets the requirements of the *jus ad bellum.*

a parliament, and how much public dialogue and deliberation is appropriate? Or is it the United Nations?

International law provides states with a right to self-defence under Article 51 of the UN Charter, but specifies that actions must be immediately reported to the Security Council, which should authorise the response and coordinate any further actions to resolve the dispute or continue the war. Thus, while understanding differing versions of state practice, international law specifies that the Security Council is the sole right authority. Chapters I and VII of the UN Charter set out a general normative prohibition on the interstate use of force, and underline the view that force is only permissible under special circumstances. The 'last resort' and 'just cause' criterion in particular are strong normative influences on UN decision-making about force, although some critics may argue that in many cases it has been a case less of 'last' than 'too late' resort. During the Cold War the Council was largely paralysed by superpower disagreement, but since 1989 has authorised force against Iraq to reverse its annexation of Kuwait, and in a number of cases (such as Libya and East Timor) has authorised the use of force to prevent or stop mass atrocities. However, in other cases, such as Rwanda, Bosnia-Herzegovina and Syria, it has failed to act or has provided weak mandates and forces. This is why the 'Responsibility to Protect' doctrine was established to provide guidance to member states in cases of severe humanitarian crises or crimes against humanity. The original *Responsibility to Protect* report, concerned by the strong potential for Security Council inaction when a permanent member wishes to protect an ally or is reluctant to risk forces, suggested that the General Assembly could try to force action, but warned of the prospect that a coalition of states could be forced to act unilaterally, undermining the Council's authority (ICISS 2001, 51). That would be a situation in which states could be forced to violate the 'right authority' principle to fulfil the 'just cause' principle of the *jus ad bellum* (see Chapter 20: The Responsibility to Protect).

In conclusion, we should recall the moral connection that the Just War Tradition draws between the *jus ad bellum* and the *jus in bello*: its insistence that both sets of rules be satisfied, and that restraint in the resort to force underpins restraint in its use. This highlights the tragedy in the UN Charter's failure to incorporate the intra-state resort to force into international law and collective security, which is starkly set out in the words of Article

2(7): 'Nothing contained in the present Charter shall authorize the United Nations to intervene in matters which are essentially within the domestic jurisdiction of any state'. Millions of people have died in intra-state wars since 1945, and terrible violations of humanitarian law have been committed with impunity, yet the international law of the *jus ad bellum* fell silent.

References and further reading

Alex Bellamy. 2006. *Just Wars: from Cicero to Iraq*. Polity.

Anthony Burke, Katrina Lee-Koo and Matt McDonald. 2014. *Ethics and Global Security: A Cosmopolitan Approach*. Routledge.

Christine Gray. 2004. *International Law and the Use of Force*. Oxford University Press.

ICISS. 2001. *The Responsibility to Protect: The Report of the International Commission on Intervention and State Sovereignty*. International Development Research Centre.

Michael Schmitt (ed.). 2013. *Tallinn Manual on the International Law Applicable to Cyber Warfare*. Cambridge University Press.

THE RESPONSIBILITY TO PROTECT

CLINTON FERNANDES

The Responsibility to Protect (R2P) refers to the responsibility of states to protect their own citizens from genocide, war crimes, ethnic cleansing and crimes against humanity, as well as from incitement in respect of such conduct. States remain primarily responsible for protecting their citizens, but the R2P principle envisages that a broad range of policy measures be open to the international community where states have manifestly failed to exercise their own primary responsibility. Where these policies involve the use of military force, R2P serves as an extension of the principles of Just War Theory. Academic research into R2P has explored the practices, rights and responsibilities of states, and the nature and extent of international authority. A Global Centre dedicated to research into, and advocacy of, R2P now exists in New York, and is complemented by a network of regional centres such as the Asia-Pacific Centre for the Responsibility to Protect in Australia.

Although its philosophical and political antecedents lie much earlier, R2P gained its first coherent conceptual footing in December 2001, when the International Commission on

The iron gate at the entrance to Dachau Concentration Camp in
Dachau, Germany, incorporating the chilling words '*arbeit macht
frei*' ('work makes [you] free'). The atrocities of the Nazi holocaust
led many in the international community to adopt the motto 'never
again', but it took another genocide, the Rwandan genocide of 1994,
before concrete steps were taken to establish the 'Responsibility to
Protect' norm.

Intervention and State Sovereignty (ICISS) – co-chaired by the
Algerian diplomat Mohamed Sahnoun and the former Australian Foreign Minister, Gareth Evans – released its report, *The
Responsibility to Protect*. In the years since, there has been significant revision, renegotiation and modification of the ICISS's ideas.
The original report by the ICISS proposed that R2P involved a
responsibility to prevent, react and rebuild. The third category
('rebuild') was dropped at the 2005 World Summit. The second

('react') continues to be the subject of energetic debate about the role of the UN Security Council in collective action.

Thus, there are two versions of R2P, and they differ quite sharply from each other. The 2005 World Summit version reiterated the international consensus as understood and supported by the overwhelming majority of the world's countries, namely that international military force may be used only pursuant to authorisation by the United Nations Security Council. The World Summit also allowed for an exception to be made for members of the African Union, who recognised a qualified right of intervention within the African Union itself.

By contrast, the ICISS report called for 'action within area of jurisdiction by regional or sub-regional organizations under Chapter VIII of the Charter, subject to their seeking subsequent authorization from the Security Council'. The reference to 'subsequent authorization' is intended to apply to cases in which 'the Security Council rejects a proposal or fails to deal with it in a reasonable time'. This was quite obviously intended to apply to the NATO bombing of Serbia, which did not receive Security Council authorisation and was described as 'illegal but legitimate' by the Independent International Commission on Kosovo.

The major problem with this form of R2P is that it conforms with great precision to the maxim of Thucydides: 'Right, as the world goes, is only in question between equals in power, while the strong do what they can and the weak suffer what they must'. In other words, it has the effect of authorising powerful states to use military force at will. It creates a new exception to a fundamental principle of international law as stated in the United Nations Charter, which is the foundational treaty of the international system. The Charter is clear that – apart from the inherent right of individual or collective self-defence (Article 51) – only the Security Council may authorise 'action by air, sea, or land forces as may be necessary to maintain or restore international peace and security', and only if it considers that 'measures not involving the use of armed force ... would be inadequate or have proved to be inadequate' (Articles 41 and 42).

Another major problem is the vast divide between the ICISS report's lofty concern for prevention of human suffering and the realities of the actions taken or avoided. For instance, the ICISS report describes the 'responsibility to prevent' as the 'single most important dimension of the responsibility to protect'. Prevention encompasses early warning, preventive diplomacy, ending impunity and preventive deployments. Yet according to rigorously documented studies, millions of children die every year from easily preventable causes, and R2P's advocates generally pass over these cases in comparative silence. For example, a study in *The Lancet* found that 'US$5.1 billion in new resources is needed annually to save 6 million child lives in the 42 countries responsible for 90% of child deaths in 2000. This cost represents $1.23 per head in these countries, or an average cost per child life saved of $887'. UNICEF's State of the World's Children report found that 'In 2007, an estimated 9.2 million children worldwide under the age of five died from largely preventable causes ... such as pneumonia, diarrhoea and malaria, ... malnutrition, poor hygiene and lack of access to safe water and adequate sanitation'. While there were also indirect causes including conflict and HIV/AIDS, 'two thirds of both neonatal and young child deaths – over six million deaths every year – are preventable'. Furthermore, power politics considerations continue to play a major role in whether R2P occurs. There is no R2P action for crimes committed against Kurds by Turkey (a NATO member), against Palestinians by Israel (a key US ally), against the people of the Eastern Congo (where Rwanda, an important Western ally, is a key player), and so on.

There is little doubt that R2P is a good idea, but – in the version promulgated by the ICISS report – it remains challenged by accusations of illegality, selectivity and cynicism.

References and further reading

Alex Bellamy. 2015. *The Responsibility to Protect: A Defence.* Oxford University Press.

Noam Chomsky. 2009. 'The Responsibility to Protect.' Lecture at the UN General Assembly. Accessed at www.chomsky. info/talks/20090723.htm [accessed 22 June 2015].

ICISS. 2001. *The Responsibility to Protect: The Report of the International Commission on Intervention and State Sovereignty.* International Development Research Centre.

James Pattison. 2010. *Humanitarian Intervention and the Responsibility to Protect: Who Should Intervene?* Oxford University Press.

UNICEF. 2014. *The State of the World's Children.* Accessed at www.unicef.org/sowc [accessed 24 March 2015].

REBELLION

NED DOBOS

During the later Roman Empire the political arrangements of earthly societies – particularly those that took the form of monarchies – were believed to have been crafted by God in accordance with the ordering of the celestial kingdom. The monarch was divinely empowered, and his subjects were divinely consigned. From the nobleman to the farmer, each individual had been assigned his place by God. To intentionally disrupt these arrangements was therefore tantamount to challenging the Creator's will, and resisting the monarch was on par with resisting God himself. To quote St Paul from the Christian Bible:

> Let every person be subject to the governing authorities.
> For there is no authority except from God, and those that
> exist have been instituted by God. Therefore whoever resists
> the authorities resists what God has appointed, and those who
> resist will incur judgment. (Romans 13:1–2, ESV)

Martin Luther (1483–1546), though willing to concede a right of passive disobedience in cases where the directives of government contravened the divine law (Luther 1962, 399), maintained that the civil authorities were not to be actively resisted or overthrown under any circumstances. For 'even if the princes abuse their power, yet they have it of God'. Fellow reformer John Calvin (1509–64) taught that a wicked king was God's way of punishing a sinful people, and that obedience was therefore owed even to tyrants.

Centuries later, philosopher Immanuel Kant (1724–1804) would take a secular route to the same conclusion. According to Kant, citizens do have rights that their rulers are morally obliged to respect. Unfortunately for the victims of abusive regimes, however, these rights are not 'coercive'. That is, the duties that correspond to the rights are not enforceable (Kant 1996, 302). To the oppressed citizen Kant delivers his moral instructions bluntly and without qualification: 'there is nothing to be done about it but obey'.

The work of John Locke (1632–1704) represented a radical break with the past in this connection. For Locke, a state has legitimate authority only on the condition that it rules with the consent of its citizens, and respects their natural rights to life, liberty and property. Moreover, Locke argued, legitimate political authority and justified rebellion are opposite sides of the same coin. If a state loses the consent of its people, or abuses their rights, it forfeits its authority and from that point can be legitimately resisted or overthrown. The upshot is that rebellion is justified, at least in principle, against any regime that does not roughly approximate a liberal democracy – a government that rules by consent and respects human rights.

Today, this is very much the dominant view. Contemporary political philosopher Michael Walzer, for example, writes: 'Given an illiberal or undemocratic government, citizens are always free to rebel, whether they act on that right or not, and whether they believe themselves to have it or not' (Walzer 1980, 215). This follows naturally from Walzer's stance on political obligation (the

The National Women's Monument in Bloemfontein, South Africa. In 1877 Britain annexed the South African Republic (SAR). The Boer inhabitants of the SAR (also known as the Transvaal Republic) chafed under British rule, which they deemed to be illegitimate. In 1880 the Boers rebelled against Britain, and defeated them in the First Anglo-Boer War (1880–81). This led in turn to the Second Anglo-Boer War (1899–1902) in which Britain finally defeated the rebellious Boers. The National Women's Monument commemorates the women and children who died in the concentration camps that were part of Britain's strategy to defeat Boer guerrillas in the Second Anglo-Boer War.

duty to obey directives issued by one's government). An individual can only be obliged to obey a state whose authority she has consented to, and consent can be registered validly only within a liberal democratic setting. According to Walzer:

> It is not enough that particularly striking acts of consent be
> free; the whole of our moral lives must be free so that we can
> freely prepare to consent, argue about consenting, intimate our
> consent to other men and women ... Civil liberty of the most
> extensive sort is, therefore, the necessary condition of political
> obligation and just government. Liberty must be as extensive as
> the possible range of consenting action – over time and through
> political space – if citizens can conceivably be bound to a strict
> obedience. (Walzer 1970, xii)

According to Walzer, then, if we do not owe it to our government
to comply with its commands, we cannot be obliged to refrain
from resisting when the state attempts to induce our compliance.
Thus, insofar as the subjects of illiberal states are under no political obligation, it stands to reason that they are 'always free to
rebel'. Walzer's attitude reflects popular sentiment. Today, few
would object morally to an oppressed people rising up against
their authoritarian rulers in an effort to win the freedoms taken
for granted by the citizens of liberal democracies. Nonetheless,
would-be rebels do not have *carte blanche*. While being subjected
to the rule of an illiberal state might be sufficient to meet the Just
War criterion of just cause (See Chapter 19: *Jus ad bellum* (Just
War Theory)), acts of armed rebellion must still be conducted
within the framework of the remaining requirements of Just War
Theory.

References and further reading

Ned Dobos. 2012. *Insurrection and Intervention: The Two Faces of
    Sovereignty*. Cambridge University Press.

Immanuel Kant. 1996. 'On the Common Saying "That May
    be Correct in Theory, but is of No Use in Practice"', in
    Kant, *Practical Philosophy*. Mary J. Gregor (trans. and ed.).
    Cambridge University Press.

Martin Luther. 1962. 'On Secular Authority', in *Martin Luther: Selections from his Writings*, John Dillenberger (ed.). Anchor Books.

Michael Walzer. 1970. *Obligations: Essays on Disobedience, War, and Citizenship*. Simon & Schuster.

Michael Walzer. 1980. 'The Moral Standing of States: A Response to Four Critics'. *Philosophy and Public Affairs* 9 (3), pp. 209–29.

The Holy Bible. English Standard Version.

HUMANITARIAN INTERVENTION

NED DOBOS

Humanitarian intervention is a term used to describe any operation with the following features:

1 It involves the crossing of international boundaries. One state or coalition ('the intervener') conducts the operation on territory belonging to another sovereign state ('the target').

2 It involves the use of coercive power or military force.

3 The operation takes place against the will of, or without the permission of, the government of the target country.

4 The purpose of the intervention is to protect the citizens of the target country against human rights violations, usually at the hands of their own government or a sub-state group backed by the government.

The fourth condition raises two key questions, which continue to generate radically divergent responses. Must a humanitarian intervention have a 'pure' humanitarian motive in play? And how severe and widespread must the human rights abuses be before foreign intervention becomes a morally legitimate option?

To the first question: When we say that the purpose of a humanitarian intervention is to protect human rights, does that mean an operation is disqualified if there are ulterior motives of a political or economic nature in play? Some say yes. As early as 1880 English jurist Sheldon Amos (1835–86) wrote that 'so far as [humanitarian] intervention is concerned ... the purity

A statue of a winged Icarus mounted on the Air Force Headquarters building in Belgrade, Serbia, which was bombed by NATO aircraft as part of NATO's humanitarian intervention in the Kosovo War in 1999.

of the motives should be conspicuous' (Amos 1880, 159). In a more recent statement, Bhikhu Parekh asserts that a humanitarian intervention is, by definition, 'wholly or primarily guided by the sentiment of humanity, compassion or fellow feeling' (Frowe 2014, 96). On this view, an intervention counts as humanitarian only if the intervener is 'disinterested' or acting purely out of altruistic concern for the victims of the human rights abuses.

If this is correct, actual instances of humanitarian intervention are likely to be few and far between. In 1973 Thomas Franck and Nigel Rodley conducted an analysis of all of the supposed cases of humanitarian intervention throughout history. Finding that the intervening party invariably had some self-interested reason for getting involved, the authors concluded that one finds no genuine examples of humanitarian intervention in history whatsoever (Franck and Rodley 1973, 278–79).

But not everyone agrees that an intervention must be purely motivated to satisfy the fourth condition identified above. An increasing number of commentators have come to accept that a military intervention can properly be described as 'humanitarian' even if it is motivated in part by political, economic and strategic concerns. The point can be made by way of analogy. Suppose you come across a drowning child and decide to rescue him from the water. If it is later discovered that you only did this to be rewarded, or to get your face in the newspaper, we might be inclined to think that you are a shallow person. But surely we would not deny that you *rescued* the child. The fact that you had a selfish motive does not affect how we characterise the act that you performed; it only affects how we judge *your character*. Why should we not take the same approach to defining humanitarian intervention, which is simply an act of rescue writ large? If the intervention will have the effect of protecting people from human rights violations, why should we refuse to characterise it as a humanitarian operation simply because the intervener had mixed motives?

A second controversy relates to how severe and widespread the human rights abuses need to be before foreign intervention becomes a morally legitimate option. In his *Just and Unjust Wars*, first published in 1977, Michael Walzer famously argues that humanitarian intervention is only justified as a response to atrocities that 'shock the moral conscience of humankind'. At the time of publication Walzer suggested that only massacre, genocide and enslavement reach this threshold of severity, but in 1980 he added 'the expulsion of very large numbers of people', or ethnic cleansing, to the list (Walzer 1980, 217–18). In all but these extreme cases, Walzer argues, humanitarian intervention is wrong in principle, on the grounds that it compromises the target community's right to political self-determination – their right to be governed in accordance with their traditions and in a way that reflects their inherited culture. A similar position can be found enshrined in the 2001 report of the International Commission on Intervention and State Sovereignty, *The Responsibility to Protect* (see Chapter 20: The Responsibility to Protect). The document states that humanitarian intervention is acceptable only in response to 'large scale loss of life' or forcible expulsion from territory.

On this view, the infringement of basic human rights does not constitute a just cause for intervention unless those rights abuses are systematic. Scattered killings in the course of 'ordinary oppression' are not enough. Moreover, the systematic violation of less basic human rights – like the right to free speech or political assembly – can never justify foreign intervention.

The contrasting position, sometimes referred to as 'cosmopolitan interventionism', says that that intervention in defence of *any* of the human rights listed under international law is permissible, at least in principle. Fernando Teson (1995) is a leading proponent of this view. If we agree that all persons are morally free and equal, Teson argues – that 'every person in the world is entitled to the same dignified treatment' – then we must agree that all individuals, regardless of the society to which they belong, are entitled to all of the rights that the world's privileged enjoy in Western liberal democracies. This includes of course the right not to be subjected to genocidal attack, but it also includes the right to dissent, free speech, religious practice, democratic participation etc. Teson and like-minded thinkers thus deny that intervention is only justified in defence of some narrow sub-set of human rights. They insist that any oppressive government that fails to honour the full complement of its citizens' rights is a legitimate target of, and provides a just cause for, foreign intervention and regime change at the hands of foreign powers. Interventions must, however, meet the remaining requirements of the *jus ad bellum* to be justified (see Chapter 19: *Jus ad bellum* (Just War Theory)).

References and further reading

Sheldon Amos. 1880. *Political and Legal Remedies for War.* Harper.

Ned Dobos. 2012. *Insurrection and Intervention: The Two Faces of Sovereignty.* Cambridge University Press.

Thomas Franck and Nigel S. Rodley. 1973. 'After Bangladesh: The Law of Humanitarian Intervention by Military Force'. *The American Journal of International Law* 67 (April), pp. 279–85.

Helen Frowe. 2014. 'Judging Armed Humanitarian Intervention', in Don E. Scheid (ed.), *The Ethics of Armed Humanitarian Intervention.* Cambridge University Press.

ICISS. 2001. *The Responsibility to Protect: The Report of the International Commission on Intervention and State Sovereignty*. International Development Research Centre.

Fernando Teson. 1995. 'The Rawlsian Theory of International Law'. *Ethics and International Affairs* 9, pp. 79–100.

Michael Walzer. 1977. *Just and Unjust Wars*. Basic Books.

Michael Walzer. 1980. 'The Moral Standing of States: A Response to Four Critics'. *Philosophy and Public Affairs* 9 (3), pp. 209–29.

ENDING WARS: JUS EX BELLO AND JUS POST BELLUM

DEANE-PETER BAKER

The question of when it is ethical for a state to enter into a war, *jus ad bellum* (see Chapter 19) has benefited from a long history of debate and scholarship. In recent times that body of scholarship has been expanded further by a flurry of work focused on issues like humanitarian intervention (Chapter 22) and, to a lesser extent, armed rebellion (Chapter 21). Largely neglected until very recently, however, has been the question of when it is ethically appropriate to end or withdraw from a war (*jus ex bello*) and the question of what a just settlement of a war looks like (*jus post bellum*).

The issue of the ethical ending of (or withdrawal from) war was almost entirely overlooked until Darrel Mollendorf published his seminal paper on the topic in 2008 (Mollendorf 2008). Mollendorf recognised the important point that war is fluid by nature, and the circumstances that make it just to commence a war can quickly change, such that it would be unjust to continue to prosecute that war even if victory has yet to be achieved. Likewise, a war might have been unjust at its start, but

Storm clouds over the Palace of Versailles in Versailles, France. The Treaty of Versailles, which officially ended hostilities between Germany and the Allied Powers at the end of the First World War, was signed here on 28 June 1919. Some scholars have argued that the treaty was unduly harsh on Germany, and may have been a contributing cause to the outbreak of the Second World War, though this is disputed.

changing circumstances could make it morally permissible (or, on a stronger interpretation, morally mandatory) for one or more parties to the conflict to continue to fight. The term *jus ex bello* is, thus, slightly misleading (though we have no better term), as it addresses not only the question of when it is appropriate to cease combat operations, but also when it is necessary to continue.

Mollendorf argues that the principles for assessing the *jus ex bello* question of whether a war should continue to be prosecuted are essentially the same as the requirements for *jus ad bellum*: just cause, likelihood of success, proportionality and last resort (Mollendorf 2008, 124). (Mollendorf sets aside the principle of right intention out of a desire to avoid his argument being distracted by any controversy over the principle, but it seems likely that he would have no objection to including this principle as well if the person making the assessment were convinced of its appropriateness.) The only *jus ad bellum* principle that requires modification is that of last resort – because the issue of *jus ex bello* only applied when a war is already underway, the question of whether the war is a matter of last resort is not a good fit. Instead, Mollendorf proposes an alternative that captures the basic moral notion inherent in the principle of last resort in a way that fits the context of a war in progress. As he writes:

> The evil of war is the reason why alternative remedies should be pursued. This is the basis for the *jus ad bellum* requirement of last resort. The same considerations provide the basis of a *jus ex bello* analogue to last resort: The war may be continued only if an alternative diplomatic remedy is unavailable. This requires not merely watching for such remedies but taking initiative to create them when the circumstances seem right. I call this *the principle of the pursuit of diplomatic remedies*. (Mollendorf 2008, 134)

If a party to a war fails to satisfy the *jus ex bello* requirement of just cause, then the ethical requirement is simple – that party must cease fighting immediately. At this point the demands of ethics shift to the manner of withdrawing from the war. This must be done in accordance with the principles of 'the minimization of casualties, of damage to vital infrastructure, and of damage to institutions required to uphold law and order'

(Mollendorf 2008, 134). If, however, a party to a war does satisfy the just cause requirement, but fails to satisfy one or more of the other principles of *jus ex bello*, then Mollendorf argues that this is a special case, one '... governed by an additional principle, namely that it must mitigate the injustices that are the basis of the just cause claim. ... [T]he path of peace in an unjust war might itself be unjust. If there is a moral requirement to mitigate injustice, which is not served by a particular policy pursued, but could have

A central tenet of *jus post bellum* is that perpetrators of war crimes must be held accountable for their actions. Where parties to a conflict are unable or unwilling to prosecute war criminals, the International Criminal Court, located in The Hague, Netherlands, has jurisdiction to do so.

been by an alternative policy, then although the war should be ended, its termination fails to satisfy a requirement of *jus ex bello*' (Mollendorf 2008, 134–35).

Somewhat more developed than the principles of *jus ex bello*, but still a relative newcomer to the scene, is *jus post bellum*. Though some guidance on the ethics of ensuring a just state of affairs in the aftermath of a war can be found stretching back through the history of the Just War Tradition, it is really only in recent times that scholars such as Brian Orend and Gary J. Bass have brought this issue into the mainstream of thought about the ethics of war. As Bass explains, in general 'just war theorists focus on the outbreak of war as a crucial moment: when state-controlled mass killing becomes morally acceptable, up to a point. But the moment at which the war ends is equally a crucial one. The return to peacetime must carry with it moral duties' (Bass 2004, 412).

Unlike the principles of *jus ad bellum* or *jus in bello*, there is as yet no clearly established and widely accepted set of principles for *jus post bellum*. Brian Orend's approach is, at time of writing, arguably the most influential. Drawing on Immanuel Kant's largely overlooked writings about the ethics of war, Orend argues that *jus post bellum* has two aspects:

> (1) that which considers those particular principles that ought to guide the conclusion of a particular war and its immediate aftermath, and

> (2) that which considers those general principles that ought to guide global institutional reform with regard to reducing the incidence and destructiveness of war itself, of war as such, over the longer term. (Orend 2000, 118)

The second of these issues is too broad to be addressed here, and Orend himself focuses on the former. He argues that the principles of *jus post bellum*, in this sense, closely follow those of *jus ad bellum*, as follows:

> *Just cause for termination.* A state has just cause to seek termination of the just war in question if there has been a reasonable vindication of those rights whose violation grounded the resort to war in the first place. Not only have most, if not all, unjust gains from aggression been eliminated and the objects of Victim's rights been reasonably restored, but Aggressor is now willing to accept terms of surrender that include not only the cessation of hostilities and its renouncing the gains of its aggression but also its submission to reasonable principles of punishment, including compensation, *jus ad bellum* and *jus in bello* war crimes trials, and perhaps rehabilitation.
>
> *Right intention.* A state must intend to carry out the process of war termination only in terms of those principles contained in the other *jus post bellum* rules. Revenge is strictly ruled out as an animating force. Furthermore, the just state in question must commit itself to symmetry and equal application with regard to the investigation and prosecution of any *jus in bello* war crimes.
>
> *Public declaration and legitimate authority.* The terms of the peace must be publicly proclaimed by a legitimate authority.
>
> *Discrimination.* In setting the terms of the peace, the just and victorious state is to differentiate between the political and military leaders, the soldiers, and the civilian population within Aggressor. Undue and unfair hardship is not to be brought upon the civilian population in particular: punitive measures are to be focused upon those elites most responsible for the aggression.
>
> *Proportionality.* Any terms of peace, ... must be proportional to the end of reasonable rights vindication. Absolutist crusades against, and/or draconian punishments for, aggression are especially to be avoided. The people of the defeated Aggressor

never forfeit their human rights, and so are entitled not to be 'blotted out' from the community of nations. (Orend 2000, 128–29)

Whether or not we accept Orend's set of principles for *jus post bellum*, or some others, what is clear is that this is an important issue that ought not to be overlooked in the ethics of war. Likewise, Mollendorf deserves our gratitude for pointing out the importance of having a principled approach to the ethics of either continuing or ending a war. If, as proponents of Just War Theory believe, war is sometimes both necessary and justified, it is essential that every possible effort is made by those who seek to wage war justly to ensure that justice is pursued in the ending of wars just as much as at their beginning or during their prosecution.

References and further reading

Gary J. Bass. 2004. 'Jus post Bellum'. *Philosophy and Public Affairs* 32 (4), pp. 384–412.

Larry May and Andrew Forceheimes (eds). 2012. *Morality, Jus Post Bellum, and International Law*. Cambridge University Press.

Darrel Mollendorf. 2008. 'Jus ex Bello'. *Journal of Political Philosophy* 16 (2), pp. 123–36.

Brian Orend. 2000. 'Jus post Bellum'. *Journal of Social Philosophy* 21 (1), pp. 117–37.

Brian Orend. 2006. *The Morality of War*. Broadview Press.

PART FIVE

THE CONDUCT OF WAR

A bullet-riddled ambulance on display outside the headquarters of the International Committee of the Red Cross in Geneva, Switzerland.

THE PRINCIPLE OF DISCRIMINATION/ DISTINCTION

IGOR PRIMORATZ

Just War Theory has traditionally been divided into two parts, *jus ad bellum* (which addresses the circumstances under which it is legitimate for a state to go to war), and *jus in bello* (which addresses the question of appropriate conduct by combatants engaged in a war). As is outlined in Chapter 23, there are also two more recent categories that have been added to Just War Theory: *jus ex bello* and *jus post bellum*. The category of *jus in bello* is comprised of two principles, the principle of proportionality (which is addressed in Chapter 26, and incorporates the principle of necessity, though that is sometimes treated as a third principle of *jus in bello*), and the principle of discrimination (or, in legal parlance, distinction).

The principle of discrimination enjoins us to discriminate between legitimate and illegitimate targets in war and to restrict our attacks to the former. That means, roughly, that our acts of war must target only enemy soldiers and military facilities, and that we must not attack civilians. Civilians enjoy immunity against deliberately inflicted harm to life, limb or property.

A minefield on East Falkland Island laid by Argentine forces during the Falklands/Malvinas War of 1982. The use of landmines is ethically problematic because these weapons are both persistent and indiscriminate and cause thousands of civilian casualties around the world every year, often decades after the conflict in which they were laid has ended.

The two main theories in the ethics of war, consequentialism and Just War Theory, offer different accounts of the grounds and stringency of civilian immunity.

In consequentialist ethics of war, civilian immunity is not primarily a matter of civilians' acts or omissions, responsibility or lack of it. It is rather a useful rule, to be adopted because adopting it has good consequences. By prohibiting the targeting of a large group of humans, it helps reduce overall killing and destruction in war better than any alternative rule or no rule at all.

This view is vulnerable to two main objections. First, the protection it offers to civilians is too weak. If all the moral force of civilian immunity derives from its utility, then it will have no such force in cases where it has no utility. There is no good consequentialist reason to comply with a moral rule in cases where compliance will not have the good consequences it usually has, and where better consequences will be attained by departing from it. This means that we ought to respect civilian immunity when, and only when, doing so will indeed reduce overall killing and destruction. But (following this consequentialist logic) whenever we have good reasons to believe that, by targeting civilians, we shall make a significant contribution to our war effort, thus shortening the war and reducing overall killing and destruction, that is what we may – and indeed ought to – do. Thus, civilian immunity becomes hostage to the vagaries of war, instead of providing civilians with protection against them.

Second, the consequentialist's view misses what everyone else, and in particular civilians in wartime, would consider the main point of civilian immunity. Think of a civilian threatened with being killed or injured by enemy fire, who is allowed to present a case against such a fate. What kind of case would she make? Surely not one in terms of the utility of the rule that says that civilians ought not to be killed or injured in war. She would rather insist that she is a civilian, not a soldier; a bystander, not a participant; an innocent, not a guilty party. That is, she would point out that she has done nothing to deserve, or to become liable, to be targeted. And she would present these personal facts as considerations whose moral import is intrinsic and decisive, rather than instrumental and fortuitous, mediated by a useful rule – a rule which under different circumstances might call for limiting the killing and destruction by targeting only 'soft' targets, that is, civilians (see Chapter 31: Terrorism). And the latter line of argument, made in personal terms, would carry greater force, and indeed be more to the point, than any impersonal balancing of good and bad consequences which would decide the issue for a consequentialist.

In Just War Theory, civilian immunity is understood as a matter of justice and rights, rather than utility. The targeting of civilians is a violation of their rights, an injustice, and wrong in itself, rather than only on account of its consequences. The civilian status doesn't in itself ground their immunity; but it is a good indication of their innocence. Civilians mustn't be attacked, because they are innocent. They aren't innocent in the sense of not being implicated in the war in any way at all. If that were the standard, in a modern war only a small part of the civilian population would qualify: those who for whatever reason (age, infirmity, anti-war views) make no contribution whatsoever to the war effort. The word 'innocent' comes from the Latin *nocere*, 'to harm'. In mainstream Just War Theory, it refers to those who are 'not harming'. All humans have a right not to be killed or injured to start with, and may be attacked only if they have waived or forfeited this right by some act or omission. One way of forfeiting this right is by joining the armed forces and fighting in war. Civilians don't do this; therefore, although they may not be morally utterly innocent in relation to war, they aren't, as Michael Walzer puts it, 'currently engaged in the business of war' (Walzer 2006, 43).

To be sure, there seem to be borderline cases. What is the standing of a soldier when he isn't performing any warlike activity because he is asleep, or on leave? What of a military chaplain? Or a medic? They don't seem to be currently engaged in the business of war; are they legitimate targets because of the uniform they wear? What of a worker in an arms factory, or a scientist doing research necessary for developing military technology? What of a member of the government that oversees the prosecution of war? They seem to be engaged in the business of war; are they nevertheless protected, because they are civilians?

Properly understood, Walzer's wording provides answers to these questions. 'Currently' shouldn't be construed as 'right now', and 'engaged in the business of war' shouldn't be construed as 'using arms in an attempt to kill, or issuing commands to someone who is doing that'. The 'business of war' is a complex, collective and prolonged activity. A soldier sleeping now will wake up later and resume his part in this business. Therefore he is a legitimate target when asleep too. The same goes for a soldier on leave. On the other hand, a badly injured soldier who is incapable of continuing to fight is considered to be *hors de combat*. This is a French term meaning literally 'outside the fight' – in the terms we have been using here, such a soldier is no longer 'engaged in the business of war'. Other combatants who are *hors de combat* include those who have been forced to parachute from seriously damaged aircraft, and those who are shipwrecked or adrift in a lifeboat.

Members of the war cabinet wear no uniform and do no fighting; but they decide that others shall fight. Therefore they are legitimate targets. Workers in an arms factory wear no uniform and do no fighting, but what they produce is necessary for fighting. Therefore they too are legitimate targets. So are scientists doing war-related research. These civilians are 'currently engaged in the business of war' and therefore don't have immunity. But the vast majority of civilians in virtually any war do. On the other hand, workers in a food factory mustn't be attacked, even though what they produce is just as necessary for a fighting army as arms. For workers producing arms provide the means of fighting and cater to soldiers as soldiers. Workers producing food help feed soldiers as human beings, not as soldiers; they cater to a need humans have at all times, not only in war. The same can be said of

The remains of the Yugoslav Ministry of Defence building in Belgrade, Serbia, which was bombed by NATO aircraft in 1999 during the NATO intervention in the Kosovo War. Such institutions usually employ significant numbers of civilian personnel, but given their close involvement in the conduct of war they are generally considered to be legitimate targets under *jus in bello.*

military chaplains and medics. They are in uniform and are often impossible to distinguish from enemy soldiers proper; but, whenever possible, they should not be harmed.

The protection of civilians proffered by the laws of war, codified in particular in the Fourth Geneva Convention (1949) and its Additional Protocols (1977), is largely in line with that enjoined by Just War Theory. However, its scope is wider, since the term 'civilians' is taken in a wider sense: it includes all those who aren't combatants, that is, take no direct part in armed hostilities. Thus, legal protection encompasses workers in arms factories, as well as political leaders who make strategic decisions concerning war.

According to the current laws of war, the military must at all times distinguish between the civilian population and combatants and between civilian objects and military facilities, and direct their operations only against the latter. Every person who is not a combatant is deemed to be a civilian; in cases of doubt, the status of civilian is to be presumed. Violence or threats of violence against civilians aiming at spreading terror among civilian population are prohibited. All attacks not directed at specific military targets, or using a method or means of combat that cannot be so directed, are deemed indiscriminate and are prohibited. Harm to civilians inflicted as a side effect of attacks on legitimate military targets must not be disproportionate to the concrete and direct military advantage sought.

Civilian immunity is obviously a highly important and very stringent moral rule. Is it absolute? Must we comply with it when that will result in losing the battle, or even losing the war? This question is discussed in Chapter 30: Supreme emergency.

The present discussion focuses on the immunity of civilians against deliberately inflicted death or injury. In war, civilians are also harmed without intent, but with foresight, as a side effect of attacks on legitimate, military targets. Ethical issues posed by 'collateral damage' are discussed in Chapter 25: Collateral damage and the doctrine of double effect.

References and further reading

David Lovell and Igor Primoratz (eds). 2012. *Protecting Civilians During Violent Conflict: Theoretical and Practical Issues for the 21st Century*. Ashgate.

Colm McKeogh. 2003. *Innocent Civilians: The Morality of Killing in War*. Palgrave.

Igor Primoratz (ed.). 2007. *Civilian Immunity in War*. Oxford University Press.

Michael Walzer. 2006. *Just and Unjust War: A Moral Argument with Historical Illustrations*. Fourth edition, Basic Books.

25 COLLATERAL DAMAGE AND THE DOCTRINE OF DOUBLE EFFECT

DEANE-PETER BAKER

As discussed in the previous chapter, the principle of discrimination requires that non-combatants not be targeted in war because they are, in the relevant sense, 'innocent' – that is, they are not engaged in the business of war and therefore not liable to be killed. The sad reality, however, is that war is a messy business and civilians and other non-combatants are invariably among the bulk of the casualties of war. In the First World War, due to the static nature of the conflict, there were relatively few civilian deaths caused by military action. Since then, however, as military forces have become more mobile and irregular forces have increasingly sheltered within civilian populations, the ratio of civilian deaths to combatant deaths has increased alarmingly. Figures from the Iraq Body Count project, for example, put the proportion of civilian casualties in the Iraq war between 2003 and 2013 at 77 per cent. While many of those deaths were the result of the deliberate targeting of civilians, and so constitute acts of murder or war crimes (depending on whether a domestic law or Law of Armed Conflict paradigm is applied), many more of those deaths were

The Möhne dam in North Rhine-Westphalia, Germany. Now rebuilt, the dam was breached on the night of 16–17 May 1943 by Royal Air Force Lancaster bombers of No. 617 Squadron as part of Operation Chastise, more commonly known as the Dam Busters raid. The flooding caused by the attack resulted in the deaths of an estimated 1600 civilians, most of them foreign forced labourers. Despite this very significant 'collateral damage', some scholars contend that the raid was nonetheless justifiable under the doctrine of double effect.

either unintended and unforeseen, or foreseen but unintended. The latter group of deaths falls into the category often referred to as 'collateral damage'.

If we are not to be pushed into either pacifism or realism then it is necessary to establish some ethical basis for dealing with the reality that it is nigh on impossible to engage in a significant armed conflict without causing any civilian casualties or causing any damage to non-military infrastructure. Here military ethicists have traditionally reached for a mechanism known as 'the doctrine of double effect'. The origins of the doctrine stretch back to Thomas Aquinas, one of the founding figures of the Just War Theory. It is not, however, a doctrine that is restricted in its use to the military context, but is a general doctrine that is employed wherever it is necessary to ascertain whether a serious harm is a permissible side effect of some course of action. The doctrine of double effect has both deontological and consequentialist elements, and consists of the following four-step test:

1   The act itself (that is, the act that will result in the harm in question) is either a good or morally neutral act.
2   The act is intended to achieve the good effect that will result, not the bad effect. The test here is a counterfactual – would the act go ahead if the bad effect were not going to occur?
3   The good effect must not be caused by the bad effect.
4   The harm caused by the act must not be out of proportion to the good that will be achieved.

Consider, by way of illustration, a fictional example that nonetheless reflects a fairly common situation in contemporary armed conflict. Imagine that intelligence reports indicated, with a high degree of reliability, that a high-value target (HVT) – in this case an influential and capable insurgent leader responsible for multiple atrocities – will be at a certain place at a certain time. Time constraints do not allow for the insertion of a Special Forces team to attempt to capture or, failing that, kill the HVT. The only targeting option available is to engage the HVT with an air-launched missile. Unfortunately the location where the HVT will be at the time when he can be targeted is in the middle of a village, and it is almost certain that some of the villagers will be killed in the strike (intelligence estimates are that there will be between five and twenty civilian casualties).

In this fictional case, is it legitimate to go ahead with the strike on the HVT? The first test, according to the doctrine of double effect, is whether or not the act itself – launching the missile at the HVT – is either a good or morally neutral act. In this case it seems clear that the answer is in the positive: the target is a legitimate target and failing to engage him now will likely result in further atrocities in the future. The second test asks whether the intentions of those ordering the strike are appropriate – is the intention to achieve the good effect, or the bad effect? In this case, again, it seems that the test is met, as the intention is clearly to kill the HVT – were it possible to kill the HVT without causing the death of any villagers, the strike would certainly still go ahead. Third, the good effect (killing the HVT) must not be a consequence of the bad effect. Again, the requirement is met – the deaths of the villagers do not *cause* the death of the HVT. Finally, the doctrine of double effect requires an assessment of proportionality – is the death of the HVT of such importance that it outweighs the harm of causing the deaths of between five and twenty villagers? This is, in this case, the hardest question to answer, as there is no hard and fast rule for weighing proportionality (for more on this see Chapter 26).

While the doctrine of double effect is widely considered to be an important means of distinguishing between permissible collateral damage and the unjustified killing of non-combatants, many analysts are sceptical about the doctrine. For some, the concern is that it places too much emphasis on intentions. While it is obviously a good thing that non-combatants are not intentionally targeted, it matters little to those who are killed, and

A Royal Air Force Lancaster bomber, the type of aircraft that was used to carry out the Dam Busters raid.

their loved ones, that their deaths were 'foreseen but not intended' rather than directly intended. So is this really a strong enough basis on which to rest a distinction between permissible and impermissible killing of non-combatants? Others are concerned that too much rests on how the act is described. In the above example, if the act is described as firing a missile at a high-value enemy combatant then that seems perfectly appropriate, whereas if the act is described as firing a missile at the village marketplace then that seems far less morally acceptable. But these are two equally plausible descriptions of exactly the same act.

References and further reading

Nancy Davis. 1984. 'The Doctrine of Double Effect: Problems of Interpretation', *Pacific Philosophical Quarterly* 65, pp. 107–23.

Iraq Body Count project. 2013. 'The War in Iraq: 10 Years and Counting' (19 March 2013). Accessed at www.iraqbodycount.org/analysis/numbers/ten-years [accessed 18 March 2015].

Lawrence Masek. 2010. 'Intentions, Motives, and the Doctrine of Double Effect', *The Philosophical Quarterly* 60 (24), pp. 567–85.

Uwe Steinhof. 2007. *On the Ethics of War and Terrorism*. Oxford University Press.

THE PRINCIPLES OF NECESSITY AND PROPORTIONALITY

ADAM C. GASTINEAU

In this chapter we will look at two *jus in bello* constraints that restrict the amount of force combatants are permitted to use during armed conflict. If the principle of discrimination determines whom we can kill and what we can break, proportionality and necessity determine the amount of damage we may permissibly do. In traditional Just War Theory these two constraints are often combined in discussion of the *jus in bello* proportionality principle. However, for greater clarity, I will pull them apart here.

Proportionality

Proportionality *in bello* is similar to the *jus ad bellum* proportionality constraint in that both require that the harm caused not be greater than the (expected) benefit to be gained as a result of that harm. The difference lies in which benefits and harms are to be considered. In *jus ad bellum* the benefits in question are those that will arise from the successful achievement of the Just Cause, and the harms are all harms that will result if the group making the calculation decides to go to war to achieve these benefits. Such

The *Enola Gay*, the Boeing B-29 Superfortress that dropped the 'Little Boy' atomic bomb on the Japanese city of Hiroshima on 6 August 1945. This attack, together with the atomic bomb dropped on Nagasaki three days later, constitute the only operational use of nuclear weapons in history thus far. Together these attacks killed, at a conservative estimate, over 150,000 civilians, with thousands more dying as a result of the nuclear fallout. Attempts have been made to justify the nuclear attacks on Japan on consequentialist grounds, but it cannot be disputed that these attacks fall catastrophically short of the *jus in bello* requirements of discrimination and proportionality.

harms include broad harms resulting from going to war: harm to the world economy, to future relations between countries, to the stability of the world political order, etc.

Jus in bello proportionality is narrower in scope. In this application, one must weigh the harms caused by some particular military action against the benefits derived from that action. So, for example, if we are concerned with determining whether or not an attack against an arms factory is proportionate *in bello*, we must compare the harms done by the destruction of the factory (death of the non-combatant workers inside the factory, destruction of surrounding civilian infrastructure or buildings and other collateral damage) to the benefits of destroying that factory (reduction in the enemy's capability to wage war, reduction in the risk that our combatants will be harmed by these particular weapons, etc.).

There are a couple of things that must be noted about this constraint. First, the moral constraint in Just War Theory is not identical to the legal constraint that exists in international law. The moral proportionality constraint factors in all harms resulting from the military act in question and compares those to the expected benefit. The legal constraint only takes into account resultant harms done to non-combatants, while constraints on harms done to combatants fall under the legal constraint of military necessity. The Just War constraints offer some grounds for this distinction, as on the face of things harms done to combatants have less effect on proportionality calculations than harms done to civilians, but often the *in bello* necessity constraint is included in the proportionality constraint, as harms to both combatants and non-combatants have an effect on proportionality.

Second, both the harms and benefits are morally weighted. This means that harms to non-combatants that result from a particular act press down more strongly against the benefits expected than harms done to combatants. Thomas Hurka has offered an interesting analysis of how this might work (Hurka 2005). He argues that when we calculate proportionality we must take into consideration not only the combatant/non-combatant status of those harmed, but also any additional duties the state might have to protect them. This means that harms that befall 'our' non-combatants have the greatest moral weight, followed by harms done to enemy ('their') non-combatants, then harms done to friendly/ our combatants, and finally harms done to enemy combatants. He points out that it may be the case that the harms done to opposing non-combatants may have equal moral weight to the harms done to our own combatants because of the moral duties of protection that a state owes to its members.

This interesting idea raises questions about collateral damage, force protection, and how much harm a state or commander might do to enemy civilians in order to protect the combatants under their command. Regardless of whether or not Hurka is correct, the constraint still forbids an agent from committing a military action that will result in greater harm than benefit if achieved. If the morally weighted harms are greater than the benefits of a particular military action, then one is not permitted to engage in that military action.

Necessity

As mentioned, the necessity constraint is often incorporated into the proportionality constraint in Just War Theory. While these two criteria are similar in the respect that they require one to weigh the harms resulting from a particular action against the benefits expected as a result of that action, they differ in an important respect. Proportionality calculations weigh the overall benefit of doing a particular action against doing nothing at all. Necessity calculations weigh two or more means of achieving a particular benefit.

The common definition of necessity found in discussion of both military ethics and the literature on ethically permissible use of force in self-defence can be summed up in the following way: A use of force is necessary, if and only if, that use of force is the least harmful means of averting the harm being threatened. At first brush this seems fairly straightforward. However, on closer examination such a principle is incredibly vague. What do we mean by 'least harmful' and harmful to whom? How are we to evaluate what means are available to the agent or agents using force? What if the least harmful means only has a small chance of averting the threat? Are we still obligated to try it before we use more harmful methods? Without further elaboration, the pre-theoretic principle of necessity leaves all of these questions open to interpretation. A clearer definition is required.

Seth Lazar has offered just such a definition:

> <u>Necessity</u>: Defensive harm H is necessary to avert unjustified threat T if and only if a reasonable agent with access to the evidence available to Defender would judge that there is no less harmful alternative, such that the marginal risk of morally weighted harm in H compared with that in the alternative is not justified by a countervailing marginal reduction in risked harm to the prospective victims of T. (Lazar 2012, 13)

Setting aside the technical terminology, this definition answers three important questions. First, it tells us that necessity calculations are to be made on the basis of the evidence available to the decision-maker. This means that when evaluating a particular act *in bello*, what matters is the evidence that was available to the decision-maker at the time the decision occurred. It also means that when choosing between two or more means of achieving a military objective, one must consider *all* available evidence, not just evidence that supports a given reasonable belief held by the decision-maker. This definition also stresses the importance of the risk of failing to avert the threatened harm. If a less harmful means significantly increases the risk of failure without reducing the risk of harm threatened, then that means can be disregarded under this definition of necessity: even when that means is less harmful than other alternatives. Finally, this definition includes all agents who might be harmed by the action, thus answering questions about which harms we should be concerned with when determining if an act does or does not fall within the necessity constraint. If my defensive act will foreseeably harm both my attacker and some bystander, I am required to include the morally weighted harms suffered by the bystander into my assessment of that means of defence.

However, Lazar argues that the individual principle outlined by this definition cannot be directly applied in warfare because of two main problems. First, it is incredibly difficult for a combatant *in bello* to do the necessary moral weighing in order to determine whether or not the harms they do in defence of themselves and their colleagues are outweighed by the harms they are seeking to avert. Second, the collective nature of armed conflict makes it impossible to apply the same constraint in both self-defence and armed conflict. Because of these two problems the necessity constraint *in bello* would need to be much less stringent than the self-defence constraint, assuming that lethal force in armed conflict is permissible. The definition is the same in both cases, but as Lazar argues, the 'collective necessity' constraint must be relaxed to allow for the fog of war and the collective nature of armed conflict.

Something must also be said about the benefits being considered under Lazar's definition of the necessity constraint *in bello*. 'Benefit' in such cases is equivalent with the military advantage gained from a particular military action. Lazar worries that defining benefit in this way would result in the necessity constraint being overly permissive: that any slight military advantage gained could justify doing a great amount of harm in order to slightly reduce the risk of failure. If we take a narrow view of what constitutes a military advantage, then this is certainly a valid concern. However, if we take a view of military advantage that makes 'advantage' relative to the just cause (thereby tying this *jus in bello* constraint to a principle of the *jus ad bellum*), equating military advantage with benefit *in bello* becomes less of an ethical concern. Doing this, however, would mean that combatants 'on the ground' would need to have a clear idea of what that just cause was so that they could effectively determine what was advantageous and what was not.

References and further reading

Helen Frowe. 2011. *The Ethics of War and Peace: An Introduction.* Routledge. Chapter 6.

Thomas Hurka. 2005. 'Proportionality in the Morality of War'. *Philosophy and Public Affairs* 33 (1), pp. 34–66.

Seth Lazar. 2012. 'Necessity in Self-Defense and War'. *Philosophy & Public Affairs* 40 (1), pp. 3–44.

Jeff McMahan. 2011. 'Duty, Obedience, Desert, and Proportionality in War: A Response'. *Ethics* 122 (1), pp. 135–67.

Jeff McMahan. 2013–14. 'Proportionate Defense'. *Journal of Transnational Law & Policy* 23 (1), pp. 1–36.

Suzanne Uniacke, 2014. 'Self-Defense, Just War, and Success', in Helen Frowe and Gerald Lang (eds), *How We Fight*. Oxford University Press, pp. 62–75.

27 SURRENDER AND DETENTION

DAVID LOVELL

At some point in a military operation, or battle, or war, there comes a point when the prospect of success of one combatant, or group of combatants, becomes small to the point of minuscule, and the prospect of their death or defeat is correspondingly overwhelming. This is the time to consider surrender, and the consequences that flow from it.

The cautious expression in the very first sentence of this chapter is due to the fact that surrender has different considerations and implications in each case: an operation; a battle; or a war. And – though it is outside the scope of this chapter – the calculation of the chances of success and failure in each of these cases, and indeed of the value of human life, is influenced by many factors including the ideological (encompassing also religious) zeal of the combatants themselves, considerations of honour, the ruthlessness and determination of the leaders of the combatants, the prospects of a civilised captivity, and simple miscalculation. Generally speaking, and explicitly in the case of the Code of the US Fighting Force (first promulgated in 1955), the circumstances under which surrender may

A farm shed employed as a makeshift prisoner-of-war camp for Argentine soldiers captured by British forces during the Falklands/ Malvinas War of 1982. The letters 'P.O.W.' can still be seen on the door of the shed.

honourably take place are when 'all reasonable means of resistance [are] exhausted and with certain death the only alternative' (Article IIc).

My primary focus here is on individual and group surrender. Surrender of one party to a war, by contrast, brings into play notions of 'conditional' and 'unconditional' surrender, reparations, and the legitimacy of the surrendering leaders and their regime, which are certainly interesting but are not germane to our present discussion as they fall under the umbrella of *jus ex bello* and *jus post bellum* (see Chapter 23). Rather than these notions, I sketch the matter of how individual and group surrender takes place, what obligations it imposes on those who openly declare to their enemy that they wish to be treated as *hors de combat* (outside combat), and the responsibilities of those to whom they surrender – at which point I turn to consider the norms and practices of detention.

Combatants who wish to be recognised as *hors de combat* have, for centuries, and for very practical reasons, raised the white flag of temporary truce in fighting in order either to negotiate a surrender of a combat group, or simply to surrender. The gesture is universally recognised, was incorporated into the Hague Conventions in 1899 and 1907, and indicates that those under its notional protection should no longer be fired upon. The other circumstances where a combatant is *hors de combat* are when he is no longer conscious or is wounded in such a way as to present no threat to his enemy and to be incapable of defending himself. Both these circumstances are explicitly recognised in international law, in the protocol of 1977 to the Geneva Convention (Article 41).

The simplicity and clarity of the gesture of surrender is muddied by the practical realities of combat, in which one combatant, determined perhaps to make a desperate final effort against an enemy who has the upper hand, may offer himself in surrender as a ruse to get close to that enemy and inflict death, even if that effort is also suicidal. This reality means that surrenders are considered with great wariness by the victors, until they are convinced that the intentions of those who surrender are genuine. It is also the reason why such a deception is considered a breach of international law (this would be a case of *perfidy* – see Chapter 29).

Nor are the actions of the victors always beyond reproach. It may be, for example, that the action preceding the surrender of their opponents has so enraged the victors that they will visit revenge upon the former; or that the obligations to care for and feed those who surrender are beyond their capability or concern; for the latter are, indeed, part of the obligations of the victors. First, that they 'recognise' the surrender and cease firing; and then to feed and care for the surrendered, including those who may require medical attention.

Those who genuinely surrender value their lives above their party's cause, however valid the latter may be. To surrender, therefore, is a reaffirmation of the value of human life which, in the modern world at least, is considered important but is constantly in tension with an approach that values 'God' and/or 'country' above all else. For both ethical and practical purposes, nevertheless, prisoners of war (POWs) are not to be punished for the mere fact of wishing to save their lives, however much they themselves may think it dishonourable (and there is no evidence to suggest that all who surrender are left with feelings of grief and guilt). Nor are such prisoners to be used as, in effect, slaves in the service of the victor. Nor are prisoners of war, in some strange parallel with ancient slavery, to be held in indefinite detention: too difficult, perhaps, to charge with any particular war crime, but considered too dangerous to be released.

These established, and widely held, injunctions against the abuse of prisoners of war are not universally held, or practised. Indeed, the most egregious abuses of them have been witnessed over the past hundred years. The Japanese treatment of POWs in the Second World War, justified by a version of their warrior code that saw any surrender as dishonourable, saw tens of thousands of Allied POWs, not to mention hundreds of thousands of dehumanised 'coolies', turned to work on the Thai–Burma railway at the cost of hundreds of thousands of lives. Japanese and German POW camps saw medical experimentation on prisoners and work until death. The examples are too numerous, and too horrific, to detail in a chapter of this size, but they should not be forgotten. It is also worth noting, if only to condemn, the psychological warfare – often called 'brainwashing' – used especially against UN troops captured by the North Koreans in the Korean War in the early 1950s, where physical and psychological conditioning by their captors divided the POWs and turned many of them into propagandists for the captors. The US Code of Conduct for soldiers, mentioned earlier, was adopted shortly after the cease-fire in the Korean War to make appropriate conduct by prison-ers themselves clear; and medical experimentation has in many countries increasingly been subject to strict ethical restrictions to ensure the informed consent of those subject to experiments. Whatever the safeguards and declaration of norms, enforcement of the Geneva Convention of 1929 related to the treatment of prisoners of war (and replaced in 1949 by a more comprehensive Convention), is highly dependent on the good will of the captors.

In recent years, especially in connection with the 'war on terror' and asymmetrical warfare more generally, a number of ethical issues have been raised about the treatment of those combatants detained by the United States. Physicians have become concerned that the cooperation of medical professionals in the force-feeding of prisoners violates medical ethics. There is widespread concern at what is generally recognised as the use of torture by US offi-cials at the prison at Guantanamo Bay (beatings, sleep depri-vation and near-drownings), undertaken on the unsafe grounds that information gained from such torture would save the lives of others who were in imminent danger. There is a fundamental concern within a society committed to the rule of law about the legal limbo of 'Gitmo' itself (on the island of Cuba but under the control of the United States, intended not just to separate prisoners of war from US soil, but also – ultimately unsuccessfully – to isolate them from the jurisdiction of US law), and a related concern about the ethics of indefinite detention of prisoners who have neither been charged with a war crime nor tried.

The issues surrounding surrender and detention are as relevant, and pressing, now as when the international community first gathered in The Hague in 1899 to attempt to formalise this area of international law.

References and further reading

George J. Annas, Sandra S. Crosby and Leonard H. Glantz. 2013. 'Guantanamo Bay: A Medical Ethics-free Zone?' *New England Journal of Medicine* 369, pp. 101–03.

Code of Conduct for Members of the Armed Forces of the United States, 1955 and revised. Accessed at www.archives.gov/federal-register/codification/executive-order/10631.html [accessed 23 May 2015].

Convention (III) Relative to the Treatment of Prisoners of War. Geneva, 12 August 1949. Accessed at https://www.icrc.org/ihl/INTRO/375?OpenDocument [accessed 23 May 2015].

S.P. MacKenzie. 1994. 'The Treatment of Prisoners of War in World War II'. *Journal of Modern History* 66, pp. 487–520.

Jessica Wolfendale. 2013. 'Psychologists, Torture and SERE', in Michael L. Gross and Don Carrick (eds), *Military Medical Ethics for the 21st Century*. Ashgate, pp. 173–92.

28 PEACEKEEPING

MESUT UYAR

Traditional (also known as classic or first generation) peacekeeping operations are deployments of mainly military personnel or troops in an interstate conflict as interposition forces with light arms or as military observers without arms. These deployments take place with the consent of the conflicting parties (especially the host country or countries) to support political and diplomatic efforts and negotiations for a peaceful settlement of a dispute by keeping them apart, patrolling conflict zones, and monitoring and verifying the implementation of a ceasefire agreement. These operations are generally authorised (or more precisely mandated) by the United Nations and are conducted under the auspices of the UN itself or another international organisation or a regional or sub-regional organisation, or an *ad hoc* coalition of willing states, in most cases led by a global or regional hegemon.

Observer missions are temporary missions with limited objectives. They are generally tasked to monitor, verify and report the implementation of ceasefire agreements between warring parties and sometimes to achieve some other limited objectives (for example, investigation of allegations, facilitation of prisoner-of-war exchange, supervision of destruction of armaments) in accordance with their mandate. The unarmed military observers – who are officers in rank, under the command of a chief military observer – operate in teams from the forward bases, which are generally stationed on both sides of the ceasefire line or buffer zone. They conduct regular and irregular ground and aerial patrols, establish stationary or mobile observation posts, control the movement of troops, weapons and military equipment, and report violations of the ceasefire. They may support or work together with an interposition force, but they do not take over the responsibility to physically separate the parties.

Interposition forces are also temporary missions, but their objectives are less bounded than observer missions. The lightly armed troops are tasked to physically separate the warring parties by establishing a barrier-like buffer zone. Normally the buffer zone is divided into small areas in which battalion-level independent and self-sufficient units are tasked to conduct armed patrols and establish checkpoints, observation posts and security cordons so as to make it impossible for the parties to attack each other without encountering peacekeepers. These forces also sometimes assist humanitarian relief efforts and reconstruction programs through the provision of equipment and capacity.

The key principles governing peacekeeping operations are those of *legitimacy, neutrality and impartiality,* and *minimum use of force.*

Legitimacy is the foremost principle of traditional peacekeeping operations. It is generally understood as arising out of a combination of the consent of the warring parties and the weight of a UN Security Council (UNSC) resolution. The fundamental idea is that warring parties will not show resistance and may even actively support the presence of peacekeepers if they perceive the operation to be legitimate. However, in practice UNSC resolutions seldom meet all the expectations of all local parties at all

A sign in Nicosia, Cyprus, indicating the area of responsibility of part of the United Nations Peacekeeping Force in Cyprus (UNFICYP), an interposition force that patrols the United Nations Buffer Zone that separates the Greek Cypriot forces of the Republic of Cyprus from the Turkish and Turkish Cypriot forces of the self-proclaimed Turkish Republic of Northern Cyprus. The UNFICYP mission, which has been in existence since 1964, is the clearest example of traditional or classic peacekeeping still in force today.

levels. Most often at the field level peacekeepers have to establish a working agreement with the low-level local actors to have at least their passive acceptance.

From the perspective of traditional peacekeeping, *neutrality and impartiality* have long been seen as inseparable and to a certain extent synonymous. As a term impartiality is active, whereas neutrality is passive. In combination these principles mean that peacekeepers must comply with the limitations jointly imposed by both parties, keep an equal distance from them and treat them equally, without making any judgment of the moral or legal standing of any side or any action in the conflict. This absence of moral judgment has been highly criticised by some scholars and commentators who advocate 'active impartiality', in which peacekeepers are deemed to have the right to react to violations of human rights.

The last principle is *minimum use of force*. According to peace-keeping theory, peacekeepers are primarily protected from harm by their legitimacy and neutrality/impartiality. They are not part of the conflict and are not deployed to force parties to come to a peaceful solution. They are under an obligation not to use force in the interest of any party. Unarmed military observers cannot threaten any side and have to depend on the active cooperation of the warring parties for their own protection. Similarly, lightly armed interposition forces are authorised to use their weapons only in self-defence.

Traditional peacekeeping was conceived to assist conflicting states which had reached a stalemate during a conventional conflict and were searching for a political solution. So understood, a peacekeeping operation occurs following a ceasefire agreement but prior to a final peace treaty. So it is a temporary consent-based operation which focuses on prevention or resumption of the conflict during political and diplomatic efforts and negotiations.

Traditional peacekeeping can only help to manage conflicts. It facilitates peaceful settlement but does not devise solutions or enforce them. Problems generally start with the formulation of mandates. The mandate is usually prepared in a climate of crisis.

Abandoned building in the United Nations Buffer Zone, Cyprus.

Its preparation involves a great deal of diplomatic negotiation and compromise. Political expediency usually takes priority over operational requirements. The mandate is therefore a document of compromise, and is often characterised by unclear and vague language which raises difficult questions of interpretation. Once agreed upon, it is unlikely the mandate will change, despite the fact that circumstances are often fluid. Historically there has been a general reluctance to reopen negotiations to change a mandate.

Sometimes warring parties have less than honourable motives for accepting a ceasefire agreement, seeing it perhaps as an opportunity for rearming and reorganisation, silencing domestic opposition and relieving international pressure. Most often, one side benefits more from the general freezing of the situation than the other. So when one side assesses that its chances for success are strong, it can restart the conflict by brushing aside the peace-keepers.

Peacekeeping is also hampered by the well-known shortcomings of the UN system (such as inflexible and slow bureaucracy, insufficient funding, severe mismanagement on the ground), as well as, in some cases, the limited quality of the forces committed by troop-contributing countries. Since the Cold War there has been a drastic shift from traditional peacekeeping to complex/multi-dimensional peacekeeping. Traditional peacekeeping, however, is still a viable option for the peaceful settlement of some conventional interstate conflicts.

References and further reading

Alex J. Bellamy, Paul D. Williams and Stuart Griffin. 2010. *Understanding Peacekeeping*. Second edition, Polity Press.

Daniel H. Levine. 2014. *The Morality of Peacekeeping*. Edinburgh University Press.

John Mackinlay (ed.). 1996. *A Guide to Peace Support Operations*. Thomas J. Watson.

29

PERFIDY AND MEANS *MALA IN SE*

RHIANNON NEILSEN

This chapter explains perfidy and means *mala in se* in the context of just armed conflicts. The *jus in bello* principle of discrimination asserts that (in most circumstances) combatants are legitimate targets of hostile engagement, whereas non-combatants (such as civilians, medical and religious personnel, employees of the United Nations and Red Cross/Red Crescent, and the *hors de combat*) are apportioned protection. Unfortunately, combatants have been known to intentionally cheat their adversary into falsely awarding them the status of non-combatants so as to gain a military advantage, therein committing one of the gravest ethical and law of war violations – perfidy.

Article 37 of Additional Protocol I to the Geneva Conventions defines perfidy as 'acts inviting the confidence of an adversary to lead him to believe that he is entitled to, or is obliged to accord, protection under the rules of international law applicable in armed conflict, with intent to betray that confidence'. Thus, a perfidious act is one that purposely deceives the adversary into believing the attacker is deserving of immunity in accordance with the Law of Armed Conflict (LOAC), but then exploits the adversary's respect of LOAC for unfair military gain. As such, perfidy has three essential elements: an offer, an acceptance, and a betrayal (Watts 2014, 147–59).

First, an attacker asks the adversary – verbally or by appearance (for example, by disguising him or herself as a civilian, or appearing to make a genuine attempt to surrender, or feigning serious injury) – to disqualify the attacker as a legitimate target of conflict, and instead afford him or her forbearance or protection in accordance with LOAC. Next, abiding by the ethical and lawful proscription of harming non-combatants, the adversary accepts the invitation by showing restraint or guaranteeing the attacker's security. Finally, in the adversary's moment of vulnerability or exposure that has been generated by granting the attacker asylum, the attacker betrays this confidence by killing, maiming or apprehending the enemy. This betrays an important trust that is one means by which to limit unnecessary bloodshed in war. Article 37 thus states that it is prohibited to 'kill, injure or capture an adversary by resort to perfidy'. It is important to recognise that immoral and illegal acts of perfidy are distinct from ruses of war, which are generally considered to be legally and morally acceptable. Although ruses are, too, acts of deception, they 'do not hinge on an enemy's compliance (by according an adversary certain protections) with the law of armed conflict' (Greene 2000, 45) only to have that observance of and confidence in just war laws betrayed.

The ramifications of perfidy affect not just the victim combatants immediately involved, but also the integrity of the Just War Tradition. Perfidious betrayals erode respect for, and the implementation of, the *jus in bello* principles and associated elements of LOAC that protect the impunity of non-combatants. Hence, perfidy endangers those who are legitimately entitled to protection in armed conflict, and, if it continues, the mandatory protection of non-combatants may cease to be respected alto-gether (Coleman 2013, 231). (A harrowing example of this was reported by a US Army Major, who, disillusioned by repeated perfidy by Iraqi insurgents in 2003, stated that 'we were 100 per cent sure that everyone to our front was enemy, and we were coming through to kill everything we possibly could' (quoted in Watts 2014, 111).) The prospect of resolving war and return-ing to peace is also degraded by perfidy. Acts of treachery in war dilute the trust and good faith between warring parties, and it is upon this confidence and sincerity of intention that armistices, ceasefires, negotiations and, indeed, the end of war depend (Watts 2014, 172). For these reasons, perfidy is ethi-cally and legally prohibited in the conduct of war, as are means *mala in se*.

Distinct from *mala prohibita*, which refers to acts that are wrong only because they are not permitted by the laws of the state, *mala in se*, 'evil in itself', speaks to conduct that is held as inherently immoral, irrespective of rules or laws governing such behaviour (Dige 2012, 319). According to Just War Theory, combatants are never permitted to resort to means or weapons *mala in se*, which category includes rape campaigns, torture, the use of weapons that produce an effect that is indiscrimi-nate and cannot be controlled (such as biological and chemical weapons), and genocide (Dige 2012, 319; Fiala 2008, 9). Thus, even if other conditions of *jus in bello* are met, combatants are forbidden from using such intrinsically evil or immoral means in warfare (Fiala 2008, 9). This is because no level of morality permits the use of means assessed to be axiomatically wicked in themselves: indeed, means *mala in se* constitute a 'shock to the moral conscience of mankind' (Walzer 1977, 107, quoted in Dige 2012, 318).

In short, perfidy is the deliberate, deceitful manipulation of

A sign marking the entrance to the mausoleum at the Ardeatine Caves site in Rome, where more than 300 civilians were massacred by Nazi troops in reprisals for a partisan attack on a column of SS troops on 23 March 1944. Most analysts agree that reprisal killings against civilians are an example of means *mala in se*.

the enemy's respect for the *jus in bello* principle of discrimination, to the end of gaining a military advantage. Means *mala in se* refer to methods and weapons that are considered *a priori* nefarious or 'wrong' in themselves. Because both are regarded as deeply unethical, combatants are required to abstain from their use in just armed conflicts.

References and further reading

Stephen Coleman. 2013. *Military Ethics: An Introduction with Case Studies.* Oxford University Press.

Morton Dige. 2012. 'Explaining the Principle of Mala in Se'. *Journal of Military Ethics* 11 (4), pp. 318–32.

Andrew Fiala. 2008. *The Just War Myth: The Moral Illusions of War.* Rowman & Littlefield.

Byron D. Greene. 2000. 'Bridging the Gap that Exists for War Crimes of Perfidy'. *The Army Lawyer,* Issues 332–37, pp. 45–52.

Michael Walzer. 1977. *Just and Unjust Wars.* New York: Basic Books.

Sean Watts. 2014. 'Law-of-War Perfidy'. *Military Law Review* 219 (1), pp. 106–75.

SUPREME EMERGENCY

STEPHEN COLEMAN

As we have seen, Just War Theory is traditionally taken to have two aspects: *jus ad bellum* (justice of war), which deals with when it is right to resort to war rather than attempting to resolve a dispute by other means; and *jus in bello* (justice in war), which deals with the conduct of those who are actually fighting the war, be they soldiers, sailors, airmen, marines, or even civilians who have taken up arms. While there is some dispute about the issue, most Just War scholars argue that the two main standards of Just War Theory, of *jus ad bellum* and *jus in bello*, are logically distinct and it is therefore perfectly possible for a war to meet one of these standards without meeting both of them. This distinction is even clearer in international law. Thus, unjust or illegal wars, which fail to meet the criteria of *jus ad bellum*, may be conducted in a justifiable manner, that is, in accordance with *jus in bello*. Similarly, wars which are justified, in that they meet the criteria of *jus ad bellum*, may be conducted in a non-justifiable manner, in that they fail to meet the criteria of *jus in bello*. However, even for those who accept the clear distinction between the ethics of *jus ad bellum* and the ethics of *jus in bello*, there are some situations where this distinction becomes distinctly blurred. Consider, for example, the following fictitious case.

The state of Rakdos has engaged in an aggressive and unprovoked attack on the state of Azorius. The government of Rakdos has publicly announced that its aim in the war is the total destruction of the state of Azorius which will include killing or enslaving everyone who lives there. The Azorians are losing the war badly and appear to be facing utter defeat, so their President, Augustin, orders the use of weapons of mass destruction against cities and towns within Rakdos to try to force a stop to the attacks.

This case illustrates, probably in the clearest form possible, what has come to be known as a situation of supreme emergency. The essential idea at the heart of what Michael Walzer calls the supreme emergency doctrine (Walzer 2006, Chapter 16), is that desperate times call for desperate measures. If the situation is dire enough, and the consequences faced are serious enough, then it will be justifiable to act in ways which would normally be prohibited. In concrete terms what this means is that a state, or perhaps a state-like entity, can ignore the usual standards of *jus in bello* if, and only if, three specific conditions are met. The first condition (which unfortunately is sometimes overlooked in discussions) is that the state must be the victim of aggression, not the aggressor. The second condition is that the victimised state must be about to be militarily defeated. The third condition is that the consequences of the victim state being defeated are so catastrophic that it is justified to use any means possible to avoid that defeat. In Just War terms what this means is that a state with *jus ad bellum* on its side can, in extreme circumstances, ignore at least some of the usual restrictions of *jus in bello*. As Brian Orend (2006, 140) notes, this is an idea which pushes the relationship between *jus ad bellum* and *jus in bello* to its limit and it is certainly not a part of international law.

A well-known thought experiment used by academics to test the concept of supreme emergency was put forward by the Oxford University scholar, Professor Henry Shue. Professor Shue asks us to imagine that a terrorist has planted a nuclear bomb somewhere in Paris, which will explode causing massive casualties if the terrorist (who has been captured) does not reveal its location. Does the notion of supreme emergency allow, in this case, for the terrorist to be tortured to induce him to reveal the location of the bomb?

There are some obvious practical problems here. Supreme emergency suggests that you can ignore *jus in bello* if the situation is serious enough, and losing would be bad enough. But how serious must the situation be and how bad must the consequences of losing be? While it is obviously not a good thing to lose a war, all wars are not equal. There are, for example, obvious differences between wars about sovereignty over territory (for example, the Falklands War of 1982) and wars waged to end (or prevent) genocide (for example, Rwanda in 1994). It seems obvious that supreme emergency, if it exists at all, can legitimately be invoked only if it is clear that the results of losing the war would include extreme and widespread violations of fundamental human rights. While states can, and do, resort to supreme emergency reasoning very easily, the conditions which must be met in order for this to be ethically justified are actually very stringent.

The first condition makes it clear that only a victim of aggression, and not a state which has launched an aggressive war, can ever reasonably claim to be facing a supreme emergency. The second condition, that military defeat must be very near, makes it clear that discarding the *jus in bello* restrictions is an absolute last resort. Thus, it will not be sufficient to have merely suffered some military setbacks or to have lost the initiative in the war. The third condition is especially important, however. In saying that supreme emergency can be resorted to only if the consequences of losing will be catastrophic, the idea is to limit supreme emergency to cases where it is clear that defeat will lead to enslavement of the population, or widespread massacres of innocent people, or even ethnic cleansing and genocide. If defeat in the war will simply mean that the defeated party will have to make humiliating political concessions, be forced to pay large reparations (even if these reparations are unjustified) or even if it will result in the loss of political sovereignty for the people of the defeated state, this is not sufficient for supreme emergency to apply.

The issues raised by supreme emergencies are definitely difficult to deal with, and perhaps the best that can be said is that people dealing with such situations must recognise that every possible option available to them will involve the violation of at least one vitally important moral principle.

References and further reading

Stephen Coleman. 2013. *Military Ethics: An Introduction with Case Studies.* Oxford University Press.

Brian Orend. 2006. *The Morality of War.* Broadview.

Michael Walzer. 2006. *Just and Unjust Wars.* Fourth edition, Basic Books.

TERRORISM

MARINA MIRON

What is meant by terrorism? The word 'terrorism' is often associated with the timeworn aphorism that 'one man's terrorist is another man's freedom fighter'. But this does not help us to understand what is unique – particularly in an ethical sense – about terrorism. This clichéd statement demonstrates that in practice what counts as 'terrorism' largely remains a matter of perspective and moral conviction. Calling someone a freedom fighter merely describes their goals, while applying the term 'terrorist' to the same person tells us about the means used to achieve them (Nathanson 2010, 19). Furthermore, when speaking about terrorism it is important to separate definition from moral assessment. Put simply, classifying an act as 'terrorist' should describe actions, rather than offer a moral evaluation. This is the only way to arrive at a morally neutral and objective definition. The defining features of terrorism will thus be action-centric, rather than actor-centric. A common view of terrorism is put forward by Bruce Hoffman, who defines a terrorist act as 'an act carried out by non-state actors who do not wear any military insignia' (Hoffman 2006, 43). But this is unhelpful in focusing on the nature of the actor, rather than in the act itself. For this reason, in order to remain analytically cogent the definition should avoid any specifications about perpetrators.

A more helpful definition of terrorism identifies it as having four characteristics:

a) it is an act of deliberate violence or a threat thereof;
b) it is used to promote a specific aim, which is often political;
c) it is directed against a certain number of people with a broader aim to convey a message to a larger group or its leaders;
d) it intentionally kills or injures non-combatants (or poses a threat of harm to them) (Nathanson 2010, 24).

The first three features of this definition could be easily applied to most violence that takes place in an armed conflict. The fourth feature is what makes terrorism stand out in comparison to violence taking place in conventional conflicts. The idea of intentionally killing innocent people, or in this sense non-combatants, is what, at first glance, makes terrorism morally unjustifiable. The international laws of war clearly prohibit targeting civilians, assuming that they are not taking part in any armed conflict. To be more precise, it is the principle of discrimination in *jus in bello* that sets such restrictions (see Chapter 24). While any military operation can lead, and often does, to civilian casualties or so-called collateral damage (see Chapter 25), this is taken to be a secondary effect that was not carried out intentionally. Every commander has to make a judgment call as to whether the military objective is important enough to risk collateral damage.

Something that is controversial about the above definition is that, so conceived, terrorism can be practised by both non-state actors (for example, Al-Qaeda) *and* by states. A good illustration would be the deliberate bombing of civilian population centres in the Second World War – the fire-bombing of Dresden in

New York City, location of the deadliest terrorist attack in history to have been carried out by a non-state group. The attack, which took place on 11 September 2001, was one of four coordinated terrorist attacks that took place that day. Al-Qaeda militants piloted two hijacked civilian aircraft into the North and South Towers of the World Trade Center, causing the towers to collapse and killing 2753 people. Today One World Trade Center, also known as 'Freedom Tower', the tallest structure in New York City, marks the spot where the two towers stood.

Germany and the nuclear attacks on Hiroshima and Nagasaki are particularly notorious examples.

From a realist perspective, as we have seen, the conduct of a state's (foreign) policy should be in accord with the state's self-interest (see Chapter 18). In the particular cases of Dresden and Hiroshima and Nagasaki, so long as these attacks contributed to Germany's and Japan's defeat, the bombings would be fully justified. Thus, despite the fact that non-combatant immunity was grossly violated, realists would not consider the act as problematic. This inevitably implies that, if realism is applied, under certain circumstances terrorism – including in the more commonly understood cases of terrorist acts being carried out by non-state actors – can be permissible.

Similarly, utilitarianism – the basic principle of which rests upon the belief that an action can be right as long as it maximises general utility (see Chapter 2: Consequentialist ethics) – arguably suffers from a similar inability to offer an outright condemnation of terrorism. Using the Dresden example, the bombings were carried out to break the morale of the German people in the hope of creating enough political pressure upon Hitler to make Germany surrender (Grosscup 2006, x–xvi). This, in turn, would lead to a peaceful settlement, arguably maximising general utility. Again it can be argued that acts that fit the earlier definition of terrorism can be morally justifiable.

Just War Theory is far less accommodating of terrorist acts. The *jus in bello* criteria of discrimination (Chapter 24) clearly forbids the deliberate killing of non-combatants, and the principle of proportionality (Chapter 26), properly applied, should minimise the foreseen but unintended killing of non-combatants. There are, however, two kinds of exceptions to these *jus in bello* principles that are argued for, that open up the possibility of 'legitimate' terrorism.

One of those 'exception clauses' is the controversial doctrine of supreme emergency (see Chapter 30). At least in theory, it might be possible for a non-aggressor state or non-state group that faced calamitous military defeat, leading to such outcomes as genocide, to resort to terrorism under supreme emergency – though as Stephen Coleman argues, there has not yet in practice been such a situation (Coleman 2013, 255).

The other potential exception to the Just War Theory rejection of the killing of non-combatants is raised by the doctrine of double effect (see Chapter 25). This allows for the generation of 'collateral damage' that is distinguishable from the intentional killings of non-combatants only by the fact that it is not intentional. This leaves the possibility that some acts that are generally considered to be terrorism could, following this doctrine, be considered to be morally acceptable. Stephen Nathanson, for instance, asks us to imagine that the 9-11 attackers wanted to target the Twin Towers as symbols of American power regardless of whether the buildings would be filled with people or not. Thus, their aim would be not to kill as many civilians as possible, but rather to destroy the buildings. Therefore, the attackers could claim that the deaths of the innocent were not intentional, that is, they were 'collateral damage' (Nathanson 2010, 96–103).

What this perhaps shows best is that there is a long-standing problem in defining 'terrorism'. This lack of clarity has also led to an ethical conundrum. While there is a broad and intuitively powerful consensus that terrorism is intrinsically wrong, most existing moral frameworks still allow for the counter-intuitive idea that some acts of terrorism could be justified upon moral grounds. Therefore, there is a strong need for a more objective definition of terrorism that can offer a clear and unambiguous basis on which to ethically condemn these acts, whether carried out by non-state groups or states themselves.

References and further reading

Stephen Coleman. 2013. *Military Ethics: An Introduction with Case Studies*. Oxford University Press.

Beau Grosscup. 2006. *Strategic Terror: The Politics and Ethics of Aerial Bombardment*. Palgrave Macmillan.

Bruce Hoffman. 2006. *Inside Terrorism*. Columbia University Press.

Stephen Nathanson. 2010. *Terrorism and the Ethics of War*. Cambridge University Press.

Igor Primoratz. 2012. *Terrorism: A Philosophical Investigation*. Polity.

32 TARGETED KILLING

ADAM C. GASTINEAU

Targeted killing is one of the most controversial tactics of modern warfare. Much has been written in ethical and legal journals on the subject, particularly as it is employed by Israel and the United States in their conflicts with non-state actors and terrorist organisations. Critics often refer to the tactic as 'assassination' or 'extra-judicial execution'. It is impossible to cover all the important positions and arguments for and against those views in this short chapter. Instead, I will merely highlight a few of the most central issues that must be considered in an ethical analysis of targeted killing *in bello*.

There are at least two ways that one agent can attempt to ethically justify killing another. The first is what is referred to as an *ex ante* justification; that is, a justification that is based in something the object of lethal force is doing or will do in the near future. In other words, this is a 'now' or 'future' focused justification. The second is an *ex post* justification. *Ex post* justifications are dependent on the object of force having done something in the past. *Ex ante* justifications work when the act of killing is a means to realising some ethically 'good' outcome. *Ex post* justifications are not outcome-focused, but work only if they are just in and of themselves. *Ex ante* justifications of killing are dependent on the target's 'liability' to be killed. In broad strokes, liability is a reason or set of reasons that allows the user of lethal force to ethically discount the interests of the person or persons being targeted. *Ex post* justifications, on the other hand, are dependent on desert. The individual in question must deserve to be punished: that is, he or she must 1) have committed some wrong in the past, and 2) the wrong committed must have been sufficiently heinous to make lethal force proportionate (McMahan 2008, 67–84).

The distinction between *ex ante* and *ex post* justifications is important because only *ex ante* justifications can be used in defensive uses of force, as the aim of such force is to act as a means to stop a harmful act that is occurring or to prevent such harm from occurring in the near future. If we are to argue that targeted killing is an ethically permissible act of war, we can only rely on *ex ante* justifications. The object of force must be sufficiently liable, on the basis of current or future actions, for us to discount his or her interests to the point that we do not wrong the object of force by killing them. The force must also be necessary and proportionate; that is, the act of targeted killing must be the least harmful means to avert a given threat, and the harm caused by the act of targeted killing must not exceed the harm prevented, or benefit gained, by the act (see Chapter 26). This distinction is also important because it seems to give us means to distinguish between acts of targeted killing and acts of extra-judicial execution. Extra-judicial execution, by definition, can only be ethically justified *ex post*, as it is a form of punishment. This does not mean that targeted killing and extra-judicial execution cannot refer to the same act, but it does

The Rio Terà dei Assassini – which translates as 'the street of assassins' or 'the street of murderers' – in Venice, Italy.

mean that Just War Theory cannot justify acts of extra-judicial execution.

As discussed in Chapters 24 and 26 there are three *jus in bello* constraints on use of lethal force. The principle of discrimination limits who can be targeted as an object of force. Proportionality restricts the amount of harm that can be done relative to the benefit achieved by means of that harm. Finally, the principle of necessity requires that we use the least harmful means available that will effectively realise the desired military advantage.

Discrimination is dependent on liability. Combatants are permissible targets precisely because we can discount their interests *ex ante*. As Michael Walzer puts it, a combatant is liable because 'he has allowed himself to be made into a dangerous man' (Walzer 1977, 145). In order to determine whether or not an act of targeted killing meets the discrimination constraint we must determine whether or not the target in question is a legitimate target under Just War Theory. However, problems arise when the nature of the armed conflict appears to be something other than 'war'. The influential theorist Jeff McMahan maintains that the distinction between combatants and non-combatants is primarily a legal distinction not a moral distinction and so evaporates in cases outside of warfare (McMahan 2009, 250). If this is true, it drastically limits the number of permissible targets. Even if we reject McMahan's claim, there remain significant challenges for those who hold the more traditional view. Michael Gross has pointed out that it could be argued that by identifying targeted individuals *by name* we are implicitly claiming that those targeted are guilty of some wrongdoing, and are therefore employing an illegitimate *ex post* justification in targeting them. This view can be countered, as Gross also points out, by seeing the targeted individual's name and history as simply a way to identify him or her as a legitimate target – a necessity in unconventional conflicts in which opponents seldom identify themselves through the wearing of uniforms and the like (Gross 2010, 100–21). But the question remains whether or not those targeted in cases that are not cases of 'warfare' are targeted on the basis of their liability resulting from their status as combatants, or because of past wrongs.

There are also concerns about whether or not acts of targeted killing meet the necessity requirement of the *jus ad bellum*. Some authors have questioned whether or not targeted killing is effective in averting the harms that it is meant to defend against. There is a plausible view that in killing off the leadership of a particular group one prolongs a given conflict. The holes in the command structure may be quickly filled by less experienced, often more fanatic members of the group one is fighting with, which may

Ford's Theatre in Washington D.C., where President Abraham Lincoln (1809–65) was assassinated by actor John Wilkes Booth (1838–65).

lead to greater violence. Killing established leaders may also be ineffective insofar as it removes them from the picture entirely, either killing them when successful, or driving them underground when not. This reduces any chance of a negotiated settlement of the conflict as one kills or drives away the exact parties with which one must deal to negotiate a peace.

Concerns about the proportionality constraint have also been raised. Targeted killing attacks often cause collateral damage, killing many civilians in order to eliminate one 'high value' target. There are also problems of uncertainty resulting from intelligence failures or simple human error. In some areas of the world cultural norms require males to openly carry weapons after they reach a certain age or else they are effectively emasculated (Ahmed 2013, 21). This makes it very difficult to determine who is liable to be killed and who isn't. Even if advances in technology reduce instances of collateral damage, these harms still factor into any proportionality/necessity calculation. There is also some evidence that targeted killing tactics employing unmanned aerial vehicles (UAVs) cause psychological harms to non-combatants living in the area the strikes are taking place. The certainty of the presence of UAVs, coupled with the uncertainty of when a missile will strike, causes great stress to the community. If and how such harms should be factored into proportionality and necessity considerations is an important issue when determining if targeted killing can be ethically justified within Just War Theory.

References and further reading

Akbar Ahmed. 2013. *The Thistle and the Drone: How America's War on Terror Became a Global War on Tribal Islam*. Brookings Institution Press.

Michael L. Gross. 2010. *Moral Dilemmas of Modern War: Torture, Assassination, and Blackmail in an Age of Asymmetric Conflict*. Cambridge University Press.

Jeff McMahan. 2008. 'Aggression and Punishment', in Larry May (ed.), *War: Essays in Political Philosophy*. Cambridge University Press, pp. 67–84.

Jeff McMahan. 2009. *Killing in War*. Oxford University Press.

Michael Walzer. 1977. *Just and Unjust Wars: A Moral Argument with Historical Illustrations*. Basic Books.

PART SIX
EMERGING
CHALLENGES

The remains of a building in Wadi Rum in Jordan which is alleged to
have been used by the British Army officer T.E. Lawrence, better known
as Lawrence of Arabia, during the guerrilla campaign he orchestrated
against Ottoman forces in the desert during the First World War.
Lawrence's campaign of irregular warfare was an exception to the rule
of conventional industrial era combat of the time, but foreshadowed the
dominance of irregular warfare that characterises the early 21st century.

EXPEDITIONARY CONFLICT

ADAM C. GASTINEAU

Expeditionary conflict, where military force is used for purposes other than defence of the state, is a developing field in military ethics. In law, the nature of these conflicts raises a question of whether or not military force should be constrained by the Law of Armed Conflict (LOAC) or the law enforcement paradigm, which demands that Human Rights Law take precedence over International Humanitarian Law. In ethics there is some question of whether or not Just War Theory can be applied to such conflicts, or if we need to apply some other ethical theory.

In expeditionary conflicts the military forces involved are generally fighting, to at least some extent, on behalf of the local populous or some sub-group of that populous. This is perhaps most obvious in humanitarian intervention or peacemaking operations, but is also true of peacekeepers and occupation forces that remain in place after a full-blown war has ended. This focus on benefiting the local populous by providing security and other aid places greater constraints on the permissible amount of force combatants are allowed to use in theatre. There are several reasons for this. The first is based in a reality about the nature of these types of conflict: it is often difficult to distinguish between combatants and non-combatants. Generally the threats faced by soldiers and marines on the ground come from non-state actors or insurgent forces which carry out military strikes and then blend back into the population. These tactics make it difficult to identify who one can target and who one can't, and makes collateral damage a likely outcome of military attempts to engage these unconventional opponents. However, because the cause that combatants are seeking to achieve involves benefiting the population of the area one is operating in, collateral damage is less permissible in expeditionary conflict for at least two reasons.

First, collateral damage is likely to reduce the reasonable chance of success of achieving the just cause. Killing those that one seeks to protect is not likely to be a successful strategy for a multitude of reasons that I do not have the space to list here. Briefly, one does not win over the populous and undermine insurgencies by killing non-combatants, even if one does so while targeting combatants.

Second, given the just cause one is seeking to achieve, harms done to civilians bear more moral weight in expeditionary conflict. As discussed in Chapter 26: The principles of necessity and proportionality, harms done to non-combatants are more wrongful than harms done to opposing combatants. This is exacerbated in expeditionary conflict as harm done to civilians decreases the benefit sought as well. Necessity demands that one use the least harmful means available to gain military advantage. Collateral damage in expeditionary conflict adds weight to the 'harm' side of the scales and reduces the weight on the benefit side, as harming civilians reduces the military advantage gained by reducing the reasonable chances of succeeding in achieving one's just cause. The proportionality constraint *in bello* is more stringent as well, given the benefit that one's use of force is meant to achieve. Collateral damage undermines this benefit as well as

A Hindu temple in Singapore. Expeditionary operations are often complicated by expeditionary forces having to negotiate unfamiliar cultural norms.

causing greater harm. As such, less force is ethically permitted in cases where one cannot clearly distinguish between combatants and non-combatants, and accurate targeting is required in cases where one can. In practice, the latter feature might mean, for example, that less discriminate weaponry which would be ethically permissible in a more conventional armed conflict, would be impermissible in expeditionary conflict.

Another of the major ethical tensions caused by expeditionary conflict is raised by the clash between one's duties to one's co-citizens and combatants, and one's duties to the populous one is meant to be defending. As pointed out in our discussion of the proportionality constraint, the harms done in armed conflict are morally weighted. Thomas Hurka suggests that examining both one's status as a combatant or non-combatant ranks these harms and the obligations one has to other members of one's political group. He even goes so far as to suggest that harms done to 'our' combatants should be as morally weighty as harms done to 'their' non-combatants (Hurka 2005, 57–66). Even if we reject this equivalence and give greater weight to harms done to non-combatants in general, it seems reasonable to grant that an individual has duties to one's co-citizens or co-combatants that one does not have to members of other political groups. These additional special duties add additional moral weight to harm suffered by our co-combatants, and bring the overall ethical value of harms to our combatants and their civilians closer together.

In conventional armed conflict this is not a serious concern. Some collateral damage is permitted, and so we are permitted to minimise the risk of harm to our own soldiers provided that such actions comply with the *in bello* necessity and proportionality constraints. However, in expeditionary conflicts these constraints are more stringent. Collateral damage is less likely to be morally permitted, and so it may be required that combatants take on a greater risk of harm to themselves to prevent harm to local non-combatants. While using artillery to destroy an apartment building containing combatants and possibly some non-combatants – rather than risking taking casualties by clearing the building floor-by-floor, room-by-room – may be permissible under some circumstances in a traditional war, it may not be in expeditionary conflict, as it would violate both the necessity and proportionality constraints.

Combatants fighting in expeditionary conflicts are also exposed to greater risk in complying with the discrimination requirement. A car approaching a checkpoint may or may not contain combatants. In order to comply with the discrimination requirement those manning the checkpoint must determine whether or not it does before they can target the vehicle. Waiting for the vehicle to approach to do so places combatants at a greater risk of harm than stopping the car at a distance by firing on the vehicle. However, because of the impermissibility of collateral damage in expeditionary conflict, this is precisely what combatants seem to be required to do.

It is commonly accepted, however, that one has obligations to members of one's political in-group. This in-group might be a state, or a political sub-group, like a nation or ethnic group. Such duties might also be due to co-members of particular institutions. Force-protection is therefore not necessarily ethically impermissible. Furthermore, during 'conventional' warfare one is fighting on behalf of one's own political group. This allows room to ethically justify both taking on a greater degree of risk, and to place others at some degree of risk, as you all will benefit from the realisation of the just cause for which you fight. In expeditionary conflict this is not necessarily the case. While the polity you belong to may realise some indirect benefit from success, the community in the area will realise the greatest benefits, and benefit directly. Does this mean that combatants are justified in taking on less risk in expeditionary conflict? Perhaps, but only to some extent: it is not sufficient to allow the high degree of collateral damage permitted in war in order to minimise the risk imposed on our co-combatants. This permission to minimise risk must be balanced against the importance of achieving the just cause for which one is fighting. How exactly we should strike this balance between acceptable risk to 'our' combatants and acceptable risk to 'their' civilians is a matter of some debate, and is one of the major questions that must be addressed when considering such conflicts.

Both the issues above are issues of *jus in bello* and as such presume that one is permitted to enter an expeditionary conflict in the first place. However, there is some question as to whether or not this presumption is permissible, and if so, when. In some cases of expeditionary conflict, the third parties are invited by one or more of the parties to the conflict to enter the conflict. In such cases it seems that legitimate authority has been satisfied, provided the party requesting aid can reasonably be said to constitute such authority. But not all expeditionary conflicts result from a request for aid. In discussion of humanitarian intervention (see Chapter 22) it is generally agreed that a state or political group that is grievously violating its citizens' rights gives other states or political groups just cause to enter into armed conflict with that group. But what kind of authority is sufficiently 'legitimate' to allow a state to violate the political sovereignty of another state or territory without that polity's permission? After all, on the face of things, such actions are violations of both treaty and conventional international law. One might argue that such intervention cannot be legitimately authorised unilaterally by one state or even a group of states from outside the region where the conflict is to occur. One might also argue that only large international institutions, such as the UN, can legitimately authorise such actions. On the other hand, it seems plausible to say that some violations are sufficiently heinous, in terms of severity of the violation, the scope of the violation, or both, to say that a sovereign political group engaging in such actions against its own members forfeits its sovereignty and so is not wronged should other political groups, individually or as a group, choose to intervene to protect the population.

Why is this discussion of legitimate authority important for our discussion of the *jus in bello* permissions granted to combatants fighting in expeditionary conflict? The answer should be fairly obvious: if one is permitted to use lethal force on behalf of some third party, one must have some authority to do so. Without such authority it is unclear why one is permitted to enter the conflict in the first place, let alone use lethal force against other combatants *in bello*.

References and further reading

Andrew Altman and Christopher Heath Wellman. 2009. *A Liberal Theory of International Justice*. Oxford University Press.

Thomas Hurka. 2005. 'Proportionality in the Morality of War'. *Philosophy and Public Affairs* 33 (1), pp. 34–66.

Patrick Mileham and Lee Willett. 2001. *Military Ethics for the Expeditionary Era*. Royal Institute of International Affairs.

Daniel Statman. 2011. 'Can Wars Be Fought Justly? The Necessity Condition Put to the Test'. *Journal of Moral Philosophy* 8 (3), pp. 435–51.

34

UNMANNED WEAPONS SYSTEMS

RICHARD ADAMS

This chapter explores some of the moral challenges associated with uninhabited aerial systems – sometimes described as 'drones'. The drone typifies the changing character of conflict, which is examined by the philosopher Tony Coady in his book, *Morality and Political Violence*. Coady observes that:

> The last quarter of the twentieth century and the beginning of the twenty first century have seen a dramatic decline in warfare understood as direct state-versus-state conflict, and a proportionate increase in other forms of warfare such as revolutionary and secessionist war; client war... [and] violent terrorist attacks like that of September 11 and the 'war on terror' it provoked and so on. (Coady 2011, 4)

Coady is not alone in recognising the changing character of war and the rise of non-state actors such as Al-Qaeda and its affiliates. For many thinkers, the acts of force which have come to characterise global conflict fall beyond the bounds of traditional Just War thinking and outside conventional conceptions of war.

To distinguish between acts of wholesale war, and acts of force which fall short of this benchmark, the philosopher Michael Walzer coined the term *jus ad vim*, which translates as 'the just use of force'. For Walzer, common sense dictates that some military acts – like drone strikes – are so limited in their scope and consequence, that it would be unreasonable to categorise them as acts of war. Compared to acts of war, the drone attack has a predictable and circumscribed outcome, and therefore is appropriately judged by the requirements of *jus ad vim* rather than *jus in bello*. The destructive impact is evidently less, and the economic burden smaller than an outright act of war. Small-scale acts of political violence are something less than acts of war, and less objectionable for this reason.

The moral distinctiveness of the drone assault turns on the probability of escalation. Assumed to be of such a small scale that it is unlikely to provoke full-scale war, the *jus ad vim* drone strike is claimed to be a proportionate response to violence or the threat of violence. In particular, the drone seems well placed to deal with the threat posed by non-state terrorists.

For the proponent of the *jus in vim* drone attack, terrorism has created a zone that is neither a zone of peace, nor a zone of war. Walzer argues that the war against terror is not addressed adequately by standard Just War Theory (Walzer 2007, 480). Daniel Brunstetter and Megan Braun describe an 'in-between space of moral uncertainty, where force is used on a consistent and limited scale, but war is not declared' (Brunstetter and Braun 2013, 89). This is, however, a controversial view rejected by many analysts. Tony Coady, for example, offers an alternative position.

Coady identifies as critical the threshold beyond which force is accepted. The use of force, he argues, should always be accompanied by 'genuine reluctance' and come as an authentically *last* resort. Coady suggests the *jus ad vim* argument is too permissive, and argues 'where it is really political violence rather than coercive diplomacy we are talking about, we do not need some more permissive theory distinct from just war thinking' (Coady 2011, 93). This insight is significant, since drones exemplify military technology and the illusion which goes hand in hand with technological advance. The false impression is that military force can be absolutely restricted and in some way antiseptic, as the terminology reflects. Ordnance is 'smart' and 'highly localised'; targets are 'serviced' in 'surgical strikes' by 'unmanned' and 'precision' weapons. Emblematic of advanced military technology, the

A RQ-2 Pioneer Unmanned Aerial Vehicle on display in the Air and Space Museum in Washington, D.C. On 23 February 1991, this particular UAV had the unique distinction of being the first unmanned vehicle in history to have enemy combatants attempt to surrender to it, while executing a fire-control mission for the 16-inch guns of the battleship USS *Wisconsin* during the Gulf War.

drone has provided part of an operational solution to the challenge of non-state terrorism. But the drone has also provoked philosophical problems both inside and beyond the declared war zone.

When flown outside declared war zones by secretive bureaus such as the Central Intelligence Agency, the operation of covert lethal drones raises significant questions. The covert drone enables killing without justification, without judicial oversight and without the informed public debate critical to the collective democratic conscience.

Philip Alston, United Nations Special Rapporteur on extrajudicial, summary or arbitrary executions, offers significant insight. In a study on targeted drone killings, submitted to the United Nations Human Rights Council on 28 May 2010, he criticised 'the displacement of clear legal standards with a vaguely defined licence to kill, and the creation of a major accountability vacuum' (Alston 2010, 3). Alston explained how the legitimate struggle against terrorism has been compromised by a proliferation of wicked acts, routinely explained away by the legal gloss of bureaucratic language, and he protested the failure of governments to 'specify the legal justification for policies, to disclose the safeguards in place to ensure that targeted killings are in fact legal and accurate, or to provide accountability mechanisms for violations' (Alston 2010, 3).

Deep-rooted within the structures and procedures of government and invisible to public scrutiny, the covert drone program is a pragmatic response to the challenges of non-state terrorism. But, unquestioned and invisible, the program is unsafely self-governing and unconstrained.

Military personnel also fly military drones, in declared war zones and against recognised military objectives. In consequence, military drones do not seem a far cry from any weapons system where lethal force is applied with precision from extended range. But military drones are different, and distinction between them and less contentious stand-off systems provokes demanding *jus in bello* questions.

A century after the industrial awfulness of the First World War, the drone seems to be redefining combat as technological carnage. Separating soldiers from bloodshed, the drone epitomises killing in modern conflict. The drone embodies killing as an emphatically remote abstracted act. Separating soldiers physically from their homicide, the drone serves at the same time to exaggerate the moral distance between combatants. This is significant since, without obvious moral commitment, warfare lacks an imperative sense of sacrifice and chivalry. This is a dangerous turn of events because war is a moral endeavour. More than a physical fight, a base slaughter or a legal figment, war is a richly moral concept.

When high ideals are sacrificed to pragmatism, the war is lost. This truism is made explicit in United States counter-insurgency doctrine (FM 3-24 / MCWP 3-33.5), where, in chapter seven, moral legitimacy is defined as critical to military accomplishment. Waged in the cause of a better peace, war demands ethical sensitivity. Without regard for moral ideals, the drone-wielding realists risk resentment, revenge and a cycle of endless conflict.

The drone is a technological advance, which represents a profound and pervasive challenge. The drone is a relatively precise weapon, and one that limits the necessity for military 'boots on the ground'. But the drone is not the means by which peace will be won, nor the means by which justice will be advanced. Our moral thinking must keep up. Drones must be understood and their application mastered, lest they become the concealed weapons of injustice.

References and further reading

Philip Alston. 2010. *Report of the United Nations Special Rapporteur on Extrajudicial, Summary or Arbitrary Executions to the United Nations Human Rights Council*. Fourteenth session, agenda item 3, United Nations document A/HRC/14/24/Add.6.

Daniel Brunstetter and Megan Braun. 2013. 'From *Jus ad Bellum* to *Jus ad Vim*: Recalibrating Our Understanding of the Moral Use of Force'. *Ethics and International Affairs* 27 (1), pp. 87–106.

C.A.J. Coady. 2011. *Morality and Political Violence*. Cambridge University Press.

Brian Orend. 2006. *The Morality of War*. Broadview Press.

Michael Walzer. 2007. 'On Fighting Terrorism Justly'. *International Relations* 21 (4), pp. 480–84.

AUTONOMOUS WEAPONS SYSTEMS

CLINTON FERNANDES

Autonomous weapons systems are unmanned, but they are not identical to unmanned, remotely controlled systems (see Chapter 34). Instead, they function independently of human control once deployed, and can acquire, track, select and attack targets without requiring humans to make the critical decisions.

Such a category of weapons often conjures up futuristic images of robots running amok and turning on their human masters, and sometimes of bonds of loyalty or jealousy between humans and robots. One need look no further than the 1920 play by Karel Capek (1890–1938) titled *R.U.R. (Rossum's Universal Robots)* (Capek 2004), in which a scientist named Rossum creates human-like machines known as robots (from the Czech word for forced labour). The robots later dominate humankind.

Uneasiness about robots overthrowing human control was captured in Isaac Asimov's classic science-fiction story 'Runaround' (Asimov 1942), which contains the famous Three Laws of Robotics: a robot may not injure a human being, or, through inaction, allow a human being to come to harm; a robot must obey the orders given it by human beings except where such orders would conflict with the First Law; a robot must protect its own existence as long as such protection does not conflict with the First or Second Law.

Yet anti-personnel landmines and automated sentry guns – while clearly not human-like machines – also qualify as autonomous weapons systems because, once deployed, they too acquire, track, select and attack targets independently of human intervention. At the other end of the current spectrum of technical sophistication, an anti-aircraft missile pursues its objective by performing rapid, complex calculations about range, velocity and trajectory.

Autonomous weapons systems pose fundamental legal, ethical and political questions for modern militaries. Military interest in such weapon systems is said to derive from three factors. First, they may reduce future operating costs, particularly those related to recruiting, training, paying and caring for military personnel. Second, they may lower the risk of both friendly casualties and non-combatant 'collateral damage' in comparison to their manned counterparts. Third, they may provide much greater military capability if a single weapons platform is able to acquire, track, select and attack targets and can do so at a speed that humans are simply unable to match.

These potential advantages are very attractive to military forces. The US Navy, for example, is working on an unmanned surface-based vehicle that can detect, identify and neutralise a mine in a single sortie. Such a naval drone would combine the whole kill chain into one integrated, autonomous system. A key challenge, if unmanned underwater vehicles are to be deployed and left in position for weeks or months at a time, is fuel. One solution, still on the horizon, may be to turn ocean sediment into fuel. Research has already begun into microbial fuel cells that generate electricity using oxygen and organic material from the ocean.

A Second World War vintage P-51 Mustang starting its engine. Late in the war the Mustang's speed enabled these aircraft to successfully engage an early autonomous weapons system, one of Hitler's 'Wunderwaffe' ('wonder weapons'), the V1 flying bomb, or 'buzz bomb'.

Formidable as these technical challenges may be, there are also daunting ethical challenges, the principal of which is how to make such weapons systems comply with the *jus in bello* principles of armed conflict discussed elsewhere in this book (see especially Chapter 24: The principle of discrimination/distinction, and Chapter 26: The principles of necessity and proportionality). It is no easy task to make autonomous weapons distinguish between combatants and civilians, and between combatants who are still active and those who have laid down their weapons or have been captured. Yet that distinction is demanded of human combatants under article 4 of the 1949 *Fourth Geneva Convention Relative to the Protection of Civilian Persons in Time of War*. Persons are 'protected' if they 'at a given moment and in any manner whatsoever, find themselves, in case of a conflict or occupation, in the hands of a Party to the conflict or Occupying Power of which they are not nationals'. To obey this constraint, autonomous weapons systems will need to be able to distinguish between active enemy combatants and those who have laid down their weapons or have been captured. Autonomous weapons systems will also have to distinguish between civilians who are taking a direct part in hostilities and civilians who are not but are nevertheless carrying weapons (for example, law enforcement personnel or hunters).

Autonomous weapons systems of this kind do not currently exist. It is sometimes said that such weapons will never exist, and that there will always be a need for a person 'in the loop' (that is, a human making the final targeting decisions) because even the best Artificial Intelligence (AI) technology will never be able to understand context. Machines are 'very good at quantitative analysis, repetitive actions and sorting data, whereas humans outperform machines in qualitative judgement and reasoning' (ICRC 2014, 1). Indeed, the ability of humans to disobey their orders is said to be an advantage, not a disadvantage. An oft-cited example is the 1983 case of Stanislav Petrov, a Soviet air defence officer who refused to believe credible reports from satellites in the Soviet space-based infra-red system that the United States had launched one and then several inter-continental ballistic missiles. A robot would not have been able to use such fine, nuanced judgments or to disobey its programming. Petrov is said to have averted nuclear war – something that a robot could not have done.

As a 'person in the loop', Petrov realised that the launch of a few nuclear-tipped missiles did not make sense, regardless of what the data from the automated satellites was indicating (Aksenov 2013).

An ethical argument sometimes made for the use of (technologically advanced) autonomous weapons is that they would have the ability (shared with remotely controlled weapons systems) to engage in extensive pre-attack surveillance by staying aloft for extended periods and enabling an attack during a brief window of opportunity. Unlike a human soldier, they would not be very concerned with taking cover and avoiding danger, and would therefore be more likely to identify the correct target than a human. The pressure of surviving combat is felt intensely by humans, who make quick decisions and often live to regret them. Autonomous weapons systems would also not be affected by emotions such as fear, revenge or anger, whereas a human soldier's emotions may lead to the commission of war crimes. Thus, some have argued, an autonomous weapon would be more likely to avoid unnecessary loss of life. However, an autonomous weapon would not have compassion, either. Nor, as already mentioned, is it clear if such a system would ever be able to assess a genuine attempt to surrender.

The possession of autonomous weapons that have greater precision than humans would make the use of such weapons more likely. And since the use of these weapons (as with remotely controlled weapons systems) occurs far from the public eye, there may not be much public opposition to their use. The potential consequence is that the death toll may mount slowly but steadily, and the domestic population does not experience the very real anger abroad.

Further ethical challenges are posed by the issue of accountability: since a robot can't be held accountable for a violation of international humanitarian law, who would? The programmer, the manufacturer or the commander who deploys the weapon in the field? As a result, there is an 'accountability gap' that requires ethical, legal and political attention. Even if international law and ethics comes down on the side of retaining human control, there is no agreement over what would constitute 'meaningful human control'. It may therefore be necessary to develop a new legal and ethical norm on 'meaningful human control'.

There is no doubt that the field of autonomous weapons systems will see extensive debate in the coming years.

References and further reading

Pavel Aksenov. 2013. 'Stanislav Petrov: The Man Who May Have Saved the World'. *BBC Russian*, 26 September 2013. Accessed at www.bbc.com/news/world-europe-24280831 [accessed 30 March 2015].

Isaac Asomov. 1942. 'Runaround', in *Astounding Science Fiction* 29 (4). Street & Smith.

Karel Capek. 2004. *R.U.R. (Rossum's Universal Robots)*. Translated by Claudia Novack-Jones. Penguin Classics.

ICRC. 2014. Report of the ICRC Expert Meeting on 'Autonomous Weapon Systems: Technical, Military, Legal and Humanitarian Aspects', 26–28 March 2014, Geneva, 9 May 2014.

Bradley Jay Strawser. 2013. *Killing by Remote Control: The Ethics of an Unmanned Military*. Oxford University Press.

36

NON-LETHAL WEAPONS

STEPHEN COLEMAN

The development and use of new technologies may raise a number of ethical issues, and this is particularly obvious when new military technologies are being discussed. The ethical issues of new technologies are not captured by simply examining the law regarding the use of such technologies, for two main reasons. One reason is that while there is an intimate relationship between the disciplines of law and ethics, the questions raised by these two disciplines are not the same; whatever the future may hold it is impossible to get a sense of what the laws governing the use of a new technology ought to be without considering the ethical issues that new technology raises.

The second reason is that the law almost inevitably lags behind the development of new technologies, so it is usually only after a new technology has actually been developed that lawmakers start to consider how that technology ought to be regulated in law. The case of non-lethal weapons (NLW) is an interesting one, however, since existing international laws cover the use of some specific types of NLW while not addressing at all the use of other types of NLW other than in general provisions which apply to all weaponry used in armed conflicts. There are many reasons why it might be attractive to equip military personnel with non-lethal weapons, particularly when those military personnel are engaged in what are sometimes called 'operations other than war', a category which includes such things as peacekeeping and peace enforcement missions, armed humanitarian interventions, and even counter-insurgency operations. However, while there are attractions in the idea of issuing NLW to military personnel, there are also a range of problematic issues.

When discussing military use of NLW, it is the principles of *jus in bello* which are of interest, that is, the principles of discrimination and proportionality. These principles have been incorporated into the Law of Armed Conflict (LOAC) in a number of ways, in that there are general principles in LOAC which ban indiscriminate and/or disproportionate attacks no matter what weapon is used, as well as treaties which ban the use of certain types of weaponry because these weapons are considered either to be indiscriminate or to cause disproportional harm, or both. Some NLW are discussed in LOAC, others are not. For example, non-lethal Riot Control Agents (RCA) are discussed in LOAC, having been banned as a weapon of war by the Chemical Weapons Convention of 1993. It is obviously possible that these weapons could be used in a discriminate and proportionate manner which would in fact reduce the harms of war. In fact, the then US Secretary of Defense Donald Rumsfeld commented on this situation, complaining in testimony to the House Armed Services Committee that 'in many instances our forces are allowed to shoot somebody and kill them, but they're not allowed to use a non-lethal riot control agent' (Knickerbocker 2003). The reason that RCAs are banned by the Convention as a weapon of war is almost certainly due to the concern that they may be used as lethal force multipliers rather than lethal force avoiders, in that they may be used in combination with the use of lethal force, thereby increasing, rather than decreasing, the lethality of the military operations in which such weapons are used.

Some types of weapons are banned for what might perhaps be thought of, for want of a better term, as 'cultural/socio-economic' reasons, in that the ban on such weapons seems to make little sense in some places or cultures but can be much more easily understood when examined from a different perspective. The

Symbols of the International Red Cross and Red Crescent in Geneva, Switzerland. The ICRC plays a key role in educating about the Law of Armed Conflict, as well as in developing new norms on emerging issues in armed conflict.

ban on permanently blinding laser weapons might fit into this category; this is an interesting case since such weapons might easily be defined by some people as non-lethal – while they clearly cause permanent harm, they do not directly kill their target. A US soldier, for example, may find it difficult to understand why it isn't seen to be disproportionate to shoot an enemy and kill them, but is seen to be disproportionate to permanently blind that same person. But in many less developed parts of the world, a blind person who does not have family who are willing and able to care for them will almost certainly be reduced to begging on the street in order to survive. Given such a future, it can certainly be argued that the difference between being shot with a bullet and being blinded by a laser is that the bullet will kill its target quickly and relatively painlessly, while the blinding laser will condemn its target to a long, slow death of suffering and starvation. When seen in these terms, the claim that permanently blinding laser weapons inflict disproportionate harm makes considerably more sense.

When the principle of discrimination is applied to the use of lethal force, it is always applied *before* the use of that force; military personnel are simply not permitted to deliberately target non-combatants. However, many advocates of NLW seem to advocate their use in a manner which applies the principle of discrimination *after* the use of force rather than before, essentially suggesting that NLW be used against everyone located in a conflict zone, combatants and non-combatants alike, then assessing after the fact who is and is not a combatant and taking additional action against the combatants while releasing the non-combatants. Such actions certainly seem problematic in terms of *jus in bello*. While the military are not routinely equipped with NLW, other armed forces, such as police officers, often are equipped with them, and the range of problems caused by the indiscriminate use of such weapons by those equipped with them certainly suggests that we ought to be very cautious indeed about proposing the indiscriminate use of NLW.

One final point is perhaps an obvious one, but is nonetheless extremely important. Many companies are engaged in various forms of research into NLW around the world and the holy grail of such research is to develop the perfect NLW: one whose effects are temporary and reversible without any medical intervention, but are unpleasant enough to ensure compliance with the directions of the user. Groups such as Amnesty International already worry about the potential for existing NLW to be used for purposes such as torture (Amnesty Internatonal 2007) so it should never be forgotten that the perfect NLW is also likely to be perfect for abuse, enabling painful punishment to be inflicted on the victim by an unscrupulous user with minimal risk of detection. Given the stressful situations which military personnel are often placed in, the risk to life and limb that they may face, and the tendency of such personnel to de-humanise their enemies, it seems a near certainty that some types of NLW would be misused by military personnel if they were to be issued with them. This is one final reason to be wary about the use of NLW by military personnel.

References and further reading

Amnesty International. 2007. *Amnesty International's Concerns about Taser Use: Statement to the US Justice Department Inquiry into Deaths in Custody.* October 2007. Accessed at www.amnesty.org/en/library/info/AMR51/151/2007/en [accessed 30 March 2015].

Stephen Coleman. 2012. 'Discrimination and Non-Lethal Weapons: Issues for the Future Military', in Igor Primoratz and David Lovell (eds), *Protecting Civilians During Violent*

Conflict: Theoretical and Practical Issues for the 21st Century. Ashgate, pp. 215–30.

Stephen Coleman. 2014. 'Ethical Challenges of New Military Technologies', in H. Nasu and R. McLaughlin (eds), *New Technologies and the Law of Armed Conflict*. Springer, pp. 29–41.

Pauline Kaurin. 2010. 'With Fear and Trembling: An Ethical Framework for Non-Lethal Weapons'. *Journal of Military Ethics* 9 (1), pp. 100–14.

Brad Knickerbocker. 2003. 'The Fuzzy Ethics of Nonlethal Weapons'. *Christian Science Monitor*, 14 February 2003. Accessed at www.csmonitor.com/2003/0214/p02s01-usmi. html [accessed 30 March 2015].

PRIVATE MILITARY CONTRACTORS

DAVID PFOTENHAUER

State use of civilians on the battlefield to support military forces and fight alongside them is routine, and dates back to ancient times: individual soldiers for hire, arguably the most ubiquitous form of historical private force, were commonplace on the battlefields of Greece, Macedonia and Sparta. Rome made use of hired soldiers to fill capability gaps in specialised areas such as archers and cavalry. In Europe, The Free Companies, and later, the *Condottieri* of Italy in the 13th and 14th centuries represented the evolution of *ad hoc* groupings of soldiers for hire into formalised economic organisations offering effective capabilities of force that could be rented, as needed, by rulers and sovereigns. Private contractors were used in the American War of Independence in 1776 and have become an established feature of the American way of war. Private soldiers were again used during colonial and post-colonial conflicts, Cold War proxy wars and post-Cold War conflicts in Africa. More recently, global attention has been focused on the prolific employment of Private Military and Security Contractors (PMSCs) in the wars in Iraq and Afghanistan where the ratio of soldier to civilian-contractor in the battlespace was 1:1.

A member of the Pontifical Swiss Guard near St Peter's Basilica, Vatican City. The Pontifical Swiss Guard are the last remnant of the famous Swiss mercenary units that came to prominence in the late 15th century.

The general debate concerning the various ethical and legal problems resulting from PMSCs in conflict is fractured, and to a degree, polarised. Authors such as James Pattison (2014), argue that the use of PMSCs by states will *always* foster inherently problematic moral and ethical dilemmas, irrespective of whether functional regulatory or accountability mechanisms exist at a national or international level. Opposing this, authors such as Deane-Peter Baker (2011) contend that if robust regulatory and accountability instruments were implemented, little moral condemnation or ethical concern could be levelled at their use, or more fundamentally, at their existence. In the middle of this debate, authors such as Elke Krahmann (2011) note that regulation and oversight alone will not be the answer to ethical problems raised by the employment of PMSCs in conflict.

There are several commonly raised areas of ethical concern regarding the employment of PMSCs in military operations. The first relates to the democratic control of force. Central to this argument is the contention that the use of PMSCs by states circumvents and clouds public awareness and oversight over the manner and extent to which PMSCs are being used. This concern is fuelled in large part by a perceived lack of regulation and accountability of the PMSC sector, and is exacerbated by the industry, which is generally reticent about public scrutiny.

The second challenge relates to the legal and moral conundrum of whether private military contractors should be understood as combatants or non-combatants (civilians) while they are deployed in conflict zones. Essentially this challenge is concerned with legal identity and whether civilians operating in defence roles during conflict can claim legal standing under international charters such as the Geneva Convention. It is worth noting the current policy development, particularly in the United States, has sought to align the legal identity of contractors in war zones with existing legal instruments such as the Uniform Code of Military Justice (UCMJ). This process is intended both to provide legal identity to contractors working alongside soldiers, and to remove the claim that the lack of accountability and regulation of contractors in conflict zones presents a critical human rights challenge.

Statue of Bartolomeo Colleoni (1395–1495) in Venice, Italy. Colleoni was an Italian *condottiero* (mercenary) leader who served the city state of Venice.

The third challenge relates to Just War Theory, particularly the question of how the privatisation of warfighting functions can violate the principles contained in *jus ad bellum* and *jus in bello*. The Just War Tradition is essentially aligned with the actions of states as legitimate actors in its assessment of just action before and during war (see Chapter 19 and Chapters 24 and 26). Those concerned about PMSCs argue that this statist foundation is fundamentally challenged by the emergence of this brand of non-state actors on the battlefield. In particular, there is much concern that the profit incentive of PMSCs has profound implications for determining the justness of a state's decision to use PMSCs in its forces when it goes to war.

A fourth significant issue that ethical theorists grapple with regarding PMSCs is the extent to which the use of PMSCs undermines existing notions of security as a public good. The state is widely understood as the only actor in the international system that may legitimately employ violence as a coercive tool. The use, therefore, of private entities, in the form of PMSCs, to prosecute traditional state-based actions profoundly challenges existing assumptions of security as a public function of the state. This challenge results from the use of private military contractors being linked with the desire for profit, rather than motivations such as civic duty (see Percy 2008). This challenge has become more visible with the use of PMSCs by weak or fragile states as alternatives to national forces to secure stability and foster peace. The morally precarious argument of 'peace through profit' resonates in this particular ethical dilemma and has fostered a lively debate about what conditions should be present to ethically justify the use of PMSCs instead of nationally constituted militaries.

The debates on the ethical challenges presented by PMSCs in war zones will continue to dominate the narrative of the privatisation of war. A recent attempt to clarify the legal standing of PMSC personnel is *The Montreux Document*, which was released in 2008. While this document details effective regulation and control, it has no independent legal force and remains, at best, an indication that norms regarding which actors are morally acceptable in war are changing gradually. Despite the profound ethical challenges of PMSCs operating on the battlefield, their presence in conflict is assured for the foreseeable future.

References and further reading

Deane-Peter Baker. 2011. *Just Warriors Inc: The Ethics of Privatized Force*. Continuum/Bloomsbury.

Federal Department of Foreign Affairs (Switzerland). 2008. *The Montreux Document*. Accessed at https://www.eda.admin.ch/ eda/en/fdfa/foreign-policy/international-law/international-humanitarian-law/private-military-security-companies/ montreux-document.html [accessed 20 March 2015].

Elke Krahmann. 2011. *States, Citizens and the Privatization of Security*. Cambridge University Press.

Sean McFate. 2014. *The Modern Mercenary: Private Armies and What They Mean for World Order*. Oxford University Press.

James Pattison. 2014. *The Morality of Private War: The Challenge of Private Military and Security Companies*. Oxford University Press.

Sarah Percy. 2008. *Mercenaries: The History of a Norm in International Relations*. Oxford University Press.

38 CYBER WARFARE

MARINA MIRON

The idea of warfare in the cyber domain, or cyberspace, was born with the emergence of the World Wide Web (or the modern Internet) in 1993. Since then the world has witnessed a number of cyber offensives, including the attacks initiated against Estonian websites in 2007 resulting from political tensions between Russia and Estonia; those that took place during the war between Russia and Georgia in August 2008; and the Stuxnet worm that infiltrated Iranian uranium-enrichment facilities in 2010.

Cyber-warfare specialist Martin Libicki defines cyberspace as 'an agglomeration of individual computing devices that are networked to one another (e.g., an office local-area network or a corporate wide-area network) and to the outside world' (Libicki 2009, 6). Nowadays, all developed states exploit the virtual space in all conceivable areas, such as finance, electricity, water, transportation, military matters, and so on. Consequently, cyberspace constitutes an important pillar of a state's infrastructure. A military's command and control networks, for instance, are highly dependent on cyberspace where its uses range from intelligence gathering to operating drones in a battle theatre. The use of cyberspace is, of course, not limited to states. Non-state actors such as insurgent groups have also shown a high degree of reliance upon cyberspace, employing it for various activities including the recruitment of new members, communication and counter-intelligence, to name but a few. In general, reliance upon cyberspace continues to grow exponentially.

Cyberspace's unlimited and unregulated nature makes cyber operations an attractive instrument of aggression. Some of the great advantages of launching a cyberattack include its cost-effectiveness and its ability to close the capabilities gap between stronger and weaker states. On the other hand, preventing such an attack (developing and reinforcing cyber-defence infrastructures) is complicated and expensive. Cyberattacks can be launched from almost any geographical location, and require significantly less time and resources than a conventional attack. Thus, cyberspace enables an attacker to overcome the spatial and temporal dimensions, and, most importantly, to remain virtually anonymous at low cost. Possibly the most significant merit of cyberattacks is their digital nature, which neither requires the deployment of a state's military, nor directly leads to any casualties. Force projection is thus facilitated, significantly reducing political pressure upon a state's leaders, unlike in conventional cases that often require large-scale commitments.

In addressing the ethics of cyberwarfare I will limit the scope of my comments to the ethics of attacks carried out against a state's structures and not constituting an auxiliary part of broader military operations (Libicki 2009, 7). From the perspective of the laws of armed conflict, only states have the legitimate authority to resort to force. Though there are arguments in favour of legitimate non-state use of force, the brief nature of this chapter means I cannot consider this issue here. Finally, to borrow from Clausewitz's concept of war, cyberwar shall be defined as an extension of political aims by means of conducting attacks in cyberspace that would constitute a threat to national security (Shakarian, et. al. 2013, 2).

So, can cyberwarfare be ethical? To answer this question, three important aspects need to be considered: just cause, proportionality and discrimination.

The first and the most crucial criterion related to the use of force by a state is a just cause, a pillar of the *jus ad bellum* requirements of Just War Theory. The modern interpretation of Just War Theory embodied in the UN Charter prohibits the use of force (or threat thereof) unless it is used in self-defence. This leads to several questions when applied to cyberwarfare. A critical question for a state being attacked is, who should be regarded as the perpetrator, that is, is the source an opposing state's military or civilian elements, or even non-state actors? And can a cyberattack be regarded as a use of force? Is it then ethical to use traditional forms of military force in retribution, or is it more appropriate to launch a counter-cyberattack?

These questions have led to states' reluctance to respond to cyberattacks due to their fear of violating the laws of war, thus leaving the attacker with effective impunity (Carr 2012, 45–46). Since such laws require states to attribute an attack to a particular foreign government, determining the perpetrator behind the attacks can become a costly and time-consuming task, and one rarely possible to accomplish. This is precisely why most defences against cyberattacks are passive in their nature, generally focused on decreasing network vulnerabilities.

In cases of conventional attack one can usually pinpoint the source of attack. If a missile is launched from a location in state A to strike a counterforce target in a location in state B, one can generally presume that state A used kinetic force against state B. Customary law has been violated, and state B then has the right to retaliate. In cyberspace, however, it is difficult to trace the aggressor and to determine their nature. If a worm or a piece of malware infects computers in various countries, it becomes extremely complicated to determine who is responsible and their location. If the attacker is a civilian, then the 'attack' should be classified a cybercrime, making the international law of armed conflict inapplicable (Singer and Friedman 2014, 73–76). In such cases, the reliance falls upon the domestic criminal law of the source country. If the attacker, however, is an agent of the state, then the victim-state might respond by invoking its right to self-defence. But what kind of response is then appropriate?

In order to adhere to *jus in bello* ethical principles during the conduct of war, a state needs to ensure that its response is proportional (see Chapter 26). In other words, the defensive action to be implemented should not create more damage (if any) than necessary. Further, the attack should be discriminate, directed only against legitimate targets (see Chapter 24). These should exclude non-state civilian objects. The problem in this case, unlike in conventional warfare, is that it is impossible to predict the consequences of a cyberattack, beyond the intended ones. The example of the Stuxnet worm is a good illustration. This cyberattack was successful in crippling its target, an Iranian uranium enrichment facility. However, the Stuxnet worm also went on to infect hundreds of thousands of computers worldwide. This is clearly problematic. It must be kept in mind, however, that no civilians were physically harmed by Stuxnet, and as such the attack can be considered as proportional, in contrast to the attacks carried out by Israel against an Iraqi nuclear research facility in 1981. This led to the deaths of 11 civilians and soldiers (Singer and Friedman 2014, 118–19).

There is, nonetheless, no plausible justification for excluding the possibility that a defensive cyberattack might produce either intended or unintended kinetic effects spilling over into the real

A captured Iraqi tank in Kuwait City, Kuwait. Technological advances mean that physical weapons like this are no longer a prerequisite for mounting an attack – attacks can instead be carried out in the cyber realm, employing nothing more than lines of code.

world. For example, a worm might infect an air-traffic control system leading to an aircraft crash in which civilians would die. In such a case, the use of defensive cyberwarfare would result in both the principles of proportionality and discrimination being violated.

While cyberwarfare might appear as more ethical than a conventional attack due to the possibility of avoiding open conflict, the discussion above demonstrates the complexities involved. While the world has not yet seen any horrifying cyberattacks, we should not underestimate the potential of this kind of warfare to cause a great amount of damage. Unfortunately, the present legal framework falls short of addressing the use of so-called cyberweapons. Many of the classical ethical norms are also challenging to apply in the case of cyberwarfare. While adjustments need to take place, cyberwarfare should remain subject to those norms already present in regard to the conduct of warfare.

References and further reading

Jeffrey Carr. 2012. *Inside Cyber Warfare*. Second edition, O'Reilly Media.

Martin C. Libicki. 2009. *Cyberdeterrence and Cyberwar*. RAND.

Paulo Shakarian, Jana Shakarian, Jana and Andrew Ruef (eds). 2013. *Introduction to Cyber-Warfare: A Multidisciplinary Approach*. Elsevier.

Peter W. Singer and Allan Friedman (eds). 2014. *Cybersecurity and Cyberwar: What Everyone Needs to Know*. Oxford University Press.

United Nations. 1945. *Charter of the United Nations*, 24 October 1945, 1 UNTS XVI. Accessed at www.un.org/en/documents/charter [accessed 21 May 2014].

CONCLUSION

DEANE-PETER BAKER

The poet and playwright Bertolt Brecht (1898–1956), who had to flee his native Germany in 1933 to avoid Nazi persecution, is often quoted as having said 'war is like love – it always finds a way'. Despite eager proclamations of 'the end of history' and 'wars to end all wars', the depressing truth is that, so far anyway, Brecht seems to have been right. War today doesn't look much like the collection of somewhat ritualised set-piece battles of the past, but it is no less bloody and destructive. As the capabilities offered by new technology continue to increase exponentially, offering as yet unimagined ways of enriching our lives, technology brings along with it (as the last few chapters of this book testify) a dark side – new and more sophisticated ways for us to inflict violence on one another. And it's not just the tools that are changing, the environment is changing too. The distinguished UNSW Canberra alumnus Dr David Kilcullen has pointed out in his influential book *Out of the Mountains: The Coming Age of the Urban Guerilla* (2013) that the major demographic trends driving our world mean that future conflicts will likely bear little resemblance to what we've experienced in places like Afghanistan. Instead of fighting in rugged mountains against independent-minded tribesmen we will find ourselves drawn into messy and complex engagements with technology-enabled, hybrid and amorphous non-state opponents, in conflicts that will take place among the crowded urban canyons and slums of the coastal mega-cities that are coming to dominate our world.

As the character (if not the nature) of war keeps changing, it is tempting to think that the ethical constraints on war that we currently recognise, which have roots going back into antiquity, are no longer relevant and need to be replaced – or else perhaps we should give up on ethics altogether. But it is the very longevity of the Just War framework that should give us reason to resist this impulse. There is no doubt that we have a great deal of work to do in order to understand how best to apply the fundamental principles of Just War Theory to the cyber domain, or to conflict environments like that described by Kilcullen – but the principles themselves, it seems to us, remain sound. In fact, it's in that very task that my colleagues and I are engaged, as are the many other dedicated and capable military ethicists from across the world that we collaborate with and learn from. Together we're attempting to weave the beginning–middle–end parts of Just War Theory into a seamless 'Just War continuum' that better fits today's seemingly endless irregular conflicts; we're trying to better understand how to ethically use new technologies in war; we're working to clarify whose responsibility the 'responsibility to protect' truly is; we're trying to understand the role that training and education in military ethics can play in preventing what are now being called 'moral injuries' ... and so the list goes on. The alternative is, to us, unthinkable: to deploy men and women into the furnace of war without giving them the understanding of what it means for them to walk out again with their heads held high. The employment of armed force is among the most serious of responsibilities, and it is vital that those who serve us, as well as society at large, understand what it means to carry out that task in as ethical a way as possible. Our hope is that this book will, in some small way, help us all to meet that weighty responsibility.

References and further reading

David Kilcullen. 2013. *Out of the Mountains: The Coming Age of the Urban Guerilla*. Oxford University Press.

CONTRIBUTORS

All of the contributors to this book are, at time of publication, members of the research and teaching team in the School of Humanities and Social Studies (HASS) at UNSW Canberra, the division of UNSW Australia that is located at the Australian Defence Force Academy (ADFA) and which is the academic service provider to ADFA. We are proud of the Cadets and Midshipmen that we have the privilege of teaching at ADFA, and are equally proud of our graduate students who come to us from all parts of the world and all walks of life. It is to our students – past, present, and future – that we dedicate this book.

Dr Richard Adams (Adjunct Senior Lecturer). A serving career naval officer, Richard is a graduate of the universities of Tasmania, New South Wales and Western Australia. As an Australian Fulbright Scholar, he researched at Yale University. He is interested in Stoicism and moral agency, as well as in ideas of institutional justice and legitimacy. His recent work has also addressed the emerging literature on moral injury.

Dr Deane-Peter Baker (Senior Lecturer). A former army officer who served in the British Army and South African Army, Deane is a philosopher who now specialises mainly in military ethics. He also teaches and writes in other areas including strategic studies and public policy. In addition to his role at UNSW Canberra Deane also holds the position of Visiting Research Fellow in the Department of Philosophy at the University of Johannesburg and is also a researcher in the Australian Centre for the Study of Armed Conflict and Society (ACSACS). He taught previously at the University of KwaZulu-Natal (South Africa) and in the Department of Leadership, Ethics and Law at the United States Naval Academy.

Dr Peter Balint (Senior Lecturer). Peter works mainly in the field of political theory, with a particular focus on the debate over toleration and multiculturalism. He is currently Honorary Research Fellow in Politics, Faculty of Humanities, at the University of Manchester, and has previously held visiting positions at Goethe University (Frankfurt am Main), the University of York, and the Australian National University.

Dr Anthony Burke (Associate Professor). Anthony is best known for work in the areas of security studies, international ethics, war and peace, and political and international relations theory. He taught previously at the universities of Adelaide and Queensland, and worked for two years as a research officer in the Australian Senate. His current interests include cosmopolitanism, new security agendas and conflicts, war and peace, security ethics, and climate change.

Revd. Nikki Coleman (PhD Candidate). An ordained minister of the Uniting Church of Australia, Nikki is currently working on a doctoral thesis at UNSW Canberra addressing the issue of military obedience, with particular reference to medical care and experimentation. She has held Visiting Fellowships at the Hastings Center for Bioethics and Public Policy (New York, USA) and Yale University, is a regular contributor to the teaching program at UNSW Canberra, and teaches bioethics at the Australian National University. Nikki is also a researcher with the Australian Centre for the Study of Armed Conflict and Society (ACSACS) at UNSW Canberra.

Dr Stephen Coleman (Senior Lecturer). Stephen was the founder of the military ethics program at UNSW Canberra. He previously taught police ethics for seven years at Charles Sturt University, and is a Senior Research Fellow in the Centre for Applied Philosophy and Public Ethics as well as a member of the ethics research team in the Australian Centre for the Study of Armed Conflict and Society (ACSACS). Stephen's unique expertise in military and police ethics (he also has done work in the field of bioethics) has led to numerous opportunities including a Visiting Fellowship in the Stockdale Center for Ethical Leadership at the United States Naval Academy and a consultancy on non-lethal weapons for the FBI.

Dr Ned Dobos (Lecturer). Ned's research specialisation is in the ethics of war and political violence, with particular interests in armed humanitarian intervention, pacifism and non-conscientious disobedience. He is currently an Adjunct Research Fellow in the Centre for Applied Philosophy and Public Ethics, and a Yale University Senior Global Justice Fellow. He has also previously been a Visiting Scholar at Oxford University's Uehiro Centre for Practical Ethics.

Dr Clinton Fernandes (Associate Professor). Formerly an officer in the Australian Army, Clinton's research falls into the

An Argentine recoilless rifle abandoned on Wireless Ridge during the Falklands/Malvinas War of 1982.

area of international relations and strategy, with a particular focus on the 'national interest' in Australia's external relations. An expert on East Timor, Clinton served as consulting historian to the film *Balibo* (2009), which was directed by Robert Connolly and starred Anthony Lapaglia and Oscar Isaac. He also participates in the Cognitive Science Group at the University of South Wales.

Dr Tom Frame (Professor). Tom is the Director of the Australian Centre for the Study of Armed Conflict and Society (ACSACS) at UNSW Canberra. A former naval officer and Anglican Bishop to the Australian Defence Force, he has served on several institutional ethics committees and published a number of books on ethics. An accomplished historian among whose distinguished projects was the biography of the late Australian Prime Minister, Harold Holt, he is also currently engaged in writing a commissioned history of UNSW and the Australian Defence Force.

Adam C. Gastineau (PhD Candidate). Currently a PhD Candidate at the Centre for Moral, Social, and Political Theory at the Australian National University, Adam is a regular contributor to the military ethics teaching program at UNSW Canberra. His main area of research is police and military ethics, and includes recent work on police discretion and cyber-surveillance, issues pertaining to duty of care, targeted killing, the permissible use of lethal force by police and military institutions, and the ethics of cyber-security. He has previously held the position of Research Assistant in the Centre for Applied Philosophy and Public Ethics.

Dr Paula Keating (Tutor and Guest Lecturer). Paula is a specialist in Immanuel Kant's practical philosophy, having completed her PhD at UNSW on that topic in 2007. She has published several papers on Kant. She contributes regularly to the teaching program at UNSW Canberra, particularly in the area of 'law, force and legitimacy'. Paula's philosophical interests also extend beyond the university – she has also been involved in teaching philosophy to children at primary school level.

Dr Lisa Lines (Lecturer). Lisa holds doctoral degrees in both History and Creative Writing, and primarily teaches in the History program at UNSW Canberra. Her research focuses on the Spanish Civil War, modern Spanish history, and women in war and revolution. She has previously taught at the University of South Australia, Flinders University and the University of Adelaide.

Dr David W. Lovell (Professor). David is currently Head of the School of Humanities and Social Studies at UNSW Canberra. David's research interests are wide-ranging and include democracy and democratisation, Communist and post-communist systems, Australian politics, the history of political thought, Marx and Marxisms, political corruption, and aspects of ethics related to armed forces and armed conflict. Since 1993 he has been a member of the Executive Committee of the International Society for the Study of European Ideas, and is co-editor of its journal, *The European Legacy*. David was a member of the

A bullet hole in the wall of a building in Kuwait City, Kuwait.

Australian government delegation to the Second Global Forum on Fighting Corruption and Safeguarding Integrity, held in The Hague, May 2001.

Marina Miron (PhD Candidate). Marina is a PhD Candidate at UNSW Canberra where she is working on the topic of counter-insurgency strategy. She is Assistant Editor for *Infinity Journal* and *The Journal of Military Operations*. Her main research interests include strategy, the thoughts of Clausewitz, cyberwarfare and irregular warfare.

Rhiannon Neilsen (M.Phil Candidate). Rhiannon is completing an M.Phil thesis on genocide prevention while also working as a Research Assistant and Tutor at UNSW Canberra. She has previously worked as an intern at the Asia-Pacific Centre for the Responsibility to Protect and was an intern and Executive Committee Member of the United Nations Association of Australia. She is a Student Ambassador for Study Canberra.

David Pfotenhauer (PhD Candidate). Formerly an officer in the South African Army, where he was Project Officer for the Future South African Army Strategy, David is working on a doctoral thesis at UNSW Canberra addressing the strategic potential of outsourcing to enable expeditionary operations in support of regional security commitments in the African context. David is also a Tutor and Research Assistant at UNSW Canberra. His research interests include the ethical and strategic implications of the employment of private military service providers, as well as issues of African security and security studies in general.

Dr Igor Primoratz (Visiting Professor). In his current research Igor focuses in particular on the ethics of war, where he works within the Just War tradition, and on terrorism, which he considers 'almost absolutely' wrong. Another central research interest at present is patriotism: How does it differ from nationalism? What are its main varieties? What are their moral credentials? Igor has also published work on the philosophy of G.W.F. Hegel, legal punishment, and the ethics of sex. In addition to being a Visiting Professor at UNSW Canberra, he is Professor Emeritus of Philosophy at the Hebrew University, Jerusalem, as well as an Adjunct Professor in the Centre for Applied Philosophy and Public Ethics, Charles Sturt University.

An abandoned military vehicle rests among wild flowers near the border between Serbia and Bosnia-Herzogovina.

Dr Mesut Uyar (Associate Professor). Formerly an officer in the Turkish Army, with service including deployments as a UN observer to Georgia and as a staff officer in Afghanistan, Mesut taught at the Turkish Military Academy for ten years before taking up his current position at UNSW Canberra. A specialist in Ottoman military history, Mesut also teaches and does research on conflict resolution, international relations and peace support operations. His other positions have included serving as an instructor and academic adviser at the Peace Support Training Center in Bosnia and Herzegovina.

ACKNOWLEDGMENTS

The material in Chapter 1: Ethical dilemmas and tests of integrity, is based on Stephen Coleman, 'The Problems of Duty and Loyalty', *Journal of Military Ethics* 8 (2009), pp. 105–15, and Stephen Coleman, *Military Ethics: An Introduction with Case*

The turret of a South African Eland 90 armoured car.

Studies (New York: Oxford University Press, 2013), pp. 4–6. The material in Chapter 8: Civil–military relations, draws on Deane-Peter Baker's paper 'Agency Theory: A New Model of Civil-Military Relations for Africa?', *African Journal of Conflict Resolution* (2007). The material in Chapter 30: Supreme emergency, is based on Stephen Coleman, *Military Ethics: An Introduction with Case Studies* (New York: Oxford University Press, 2013), pp. 250–53. Chapter 36: Non-lethal weapons, draws in part on material from three previously published sources: Stephen Coleman, 'Discrimination and Non-Lethal Weapons: Issues for the Future Military', in I. Primoratz and D. Lovell (eds), *Protecting Civilians During Violent Conflict: Theoretical and Practical Issues for the 21st Century* (London: Ashgate, 2012); Stephen Coleman, 'Ethical Challenges of New Military Technologies', in H. Nasu and R. McLaughlin (eds), *New Technologies and the Law of Armed Conflict* (The Hague: Springer, 2014); and Stephen Coleman, *Military Ethics: An Introduction with Case Studies* (New York: Oxford University Press, 2013).

INDEX

Printed in the USA
CPSIA information can be obtained
at www.ICGtesting.com
BVHW040036140823
668496BV00001B/62